The Inclusive Leader Scoreca

'Dev Modi provides an authentic and ... provide an empowering vision of diversity and inclusion. From his personal stories, he articulates the importance of how people from different backgrounds can feel a sense of pride in being integrated within an organisation, without feeling they have to leave their identity behind. This is a must-read for business leaders who are looking to understand the merits of inclusion and diversity and make a tangible difference.'

— **Lord Popat**, Conservative Peer and former Business and Transport Minister

'Velocity of change is a major challenge for businesses and leaders. Speed of informed decision-making is a competitive advantage in meeting that challenge. The insights and framework of 'The Inclusive Leader Scorecard' can increase the speed at which a leader understands how to build an inclusive culture and unlock the business success that follows.'

— **Rick Martino**, Independent HR Expert, Former Chief Human Resource Officer, Bose Corporation

'To use one of Dev's metaphors, we are all invited to the I&D party, but we don't know how to dance, and our impact to date is limited. Dev provides us with the steps to take, and how to bring I&D to live in our organisations, together with our teams. A huge side benefit is through his suggestions, we get to understand ourselves and our team members better, the people we dance with. A must-read.'

— **Ad Boon**, Independent Coach Expert, Former Senior VP of HR for Philips and Qatar Airways

'The Inclusive Leader Scorecard is an indispensable guide for all leaders. It provides a comprehensive, evidence-based explanation as to why matters of inclusion and equity envelop everything that is leadership and demystifies many of the concepts and much of the language that can land this agenda on the 'too hard' pile. But beyond that, the Inclusive Leader Scorecard offers a range of guided reflections, all together in one place and in a clear and structured way, that enable readers to take pragmatic steps towards their personal growth. I can see how this book could quickly

become my 'go-to' reference point, to keep my own and our organisation's cultural development headed in the right direction.'
— **Hannah Leach**, Vice President, Culture and Learning, Carnival UK

'For anyone that wants to understand more about diversity and inclusion and its barriers, this book is essential. It is simple and effective, explaining diversity and inclusion from a personal development perspective as well as how to lead the organisation. It challenges where you are now, where you want to be and how to get there. A positive and supportive tool to help make yourself and your organisation more inclusive.'
— **Jade Green**, Diversity and Inclusion Manager, Marks and Spencers

'Inclusive Leadership is not a book that just informs, if you commit to its roadmap, it can be transformative. Dev requires you not to just sit back and read but to challenge yourself to adopt the steps needed to become an inclusive leader.'
— **Frank Douglas**, CEO, Caerus Executive, Chartered Companion CIPD

'If you want an easy-to-understand and comprehensive framework then the Inclusive Leadership Scorecard is an essential read. It pulls together theory and practice into a pragmatic approach to developing your inclusive leadership skills.'
— **Jiten Patel**, Conscious Inclusion Thought Leader and author of 'Demystifying Diversity'.

'Dev's book is a timely contribution to an emergent dilemma for leaders who now need to respond to issues of diversity and inclusion but struggle to know where or how to begin. We realise organisational consciousness needs to evolve, but the whole topic becomes so tricky and laden with taboos, that inertia, (or doing nothing), becomes a risky yet likely outcome. Dev builds here the business case and logic for action, plus offers models, principles, and methods to help readers get started. As a leader, whether you are simply or even committed to tackle these issues, The Inclusive Leader Scorecard is a positive place to begin.'
— **Julie Starr**, Acclaimed Author and Entrepreneur, The Coaching Manual, The Mentoring Manual, Brilliant Coaching

'Dev's new book is a hugely valuable tool for all leaders looking to develop their inclusive leadership skills. Not only is it a very helpful summary of much of the research and theory around inclusion, but it also provides practical advice for leaders. His Inclusive Leadership Scorecard provides a fantastic framework for assessing the current state of inclusive leadership practices as well as a guide for future activity. I would recommend this book for all leaders and leadership teams looking to create inclusive organisations.'
— **Jane Welsh**, Founder and Director, The Diversity Project

'The Inclusive Leader Scorecard takes the reader through a journey of self-discovery highlighting the beliefs, values and mindsets necessary to enable inclusive teams, grow an inclusive culture and deliver an inclusive brand. Reading this book will empower leaders to activate change and accelerate progress through some accessible and insightful examples, activities and sequential steps. Inspiring, clear and packed with opportunities for self-reflection, this book will enable anybody who is driven by purpose and is looking to weave an inclusion and diversity thread into the fabric of their culture and organisation.'
— **Tea Colaianni**, Founder and Chair, WiHTL, Senior Independent Director, Watches of Switzerland

Dev Modi is a true thought leader in the I&D space. He translates complex ideas into practical and accessible information for leaders. In this book he does just that, providing a practical framework and scorecard to help leaders, teams and organisations become more inclusive. There has never been a more critical time for organisations to focus on inclusivity, and Dev's advice will help you on the journey.'
— **Katie Jacobs**, Senior Stakeholder Lead, CIPD

The Inclusive Leader Scorecard

The Definitive Guide to Unlocking the Power of Diversity

Dev Modi C.Psychol. MSc.

The Omega Academy Press

Published by: The Omega Academy Press
The Omega Academy Ltd
1 Colmer Place, Harrow, Middlesex
London, UK

The moral right of Devesh Modi has been asserted.
First published in Great Britain in 2020 by The Omega Academy Press.

ISBN: 978-1-8383248-0-3 (print)
ISBN: 978-1-8383248-1-0 (PDF)
ISBN: 978-1-8383248-2-7 (ePub)
ISBN: 978-1-8383248-3-4 (hardback)

British Library Cataloguing in Publication Data
A catalogue record for this book is available from the British Library.

For Madhav & Mum

I dedicate this book to my mum who represents a
generation that went through more hardships than
I can imagine but who persevered with optimism and
gratitude to create the opportunities I benefitted from.

I dedicate this book to my son, who represents the next
generation of leaders to whom we have a duty to leave
this world in a better place than we found it.

Thank you for teaching me both the wisdom
of history and hope in a bright future.

Contents

Acknowledgements

It was during the summer of 2020, while in lockdown on the Spanish coast, I decided to finally get my ideas about inclusive leadership down on paper. I didn't know where the words would take me, but I knew I needed to extract something positive from the challenges of our time.

Firstly, I would like to thank my mum and dad who both supported my pursuit of business psychology and allowed me to flourish. They continue to encourage and guide me to share what I know with others and to believe in myself. I thank my wife for inspiring me to write and share what I know without fear or hesitation.

Along the way, I have had the privilege of working with and learning from an array of inspirational teachers, mentors and friends.

I would like to thank my spiritual teachers, Srila Prabhupad, Tribhuvanath Prabhu and Radhanath Swami. I was introduced to Eastern wisdom and psychology through their words and books and deepened my philosophical understanding of what inclusion means. I am grateful to Paul Gilbert, Martin Seligman, Russ Harris, Stephen Covey, David Deida, Byron Katie and many other authors who have shaped me as a person.

I would like to acknowledge Jiten Patel for his insights and feedback in fine tuning my ideas along the way; those late night calls were appreciated. Thank you to Sandra Cain for her input and guidance in the book writing process; this was invaluable. I appreciate the razor-sharp eye for detail Ian Randle provided, which further enhanced the impact of my words. Finally, I am grateful to my dear friend JD, also known as the Smiling Monk, who has always encouraged me with kindness and shown me the true meaning of courage as he continues to smile in the face of ongoing cancer treatment.

About the Author

Dev Modi has worked extensively in the leadership space in a range of industries and sectors both within the UK and globally, including the Middle East and North America. He has held senior roles such as Head of Inclusive Leadership at YSC Consulting, Head of Coaching at Grant Thornton and Senior Business Psychologist at the BBC. He is currently a Partner at Equiida, a leadership advisory business dedicated to inclusion, innovation and improving performance of major companies, globally.

Dev's core areas of expertise are inclusion and diversity, inclusive leadership, leadership assessment and culture change. He currently works and lives in two cities, London and Malaga. He regularly volunteers his time to deliver personal development workshops to members of the public to raise funds for charitable causes close to his heart.

Dev is a graduate of The London School of Economics and Political Science with a Bachelors in Management Science. He has a Masters in Organisational Psychology from City University. He is an Associate Fellow and Chartered Member of The British Psychological Society.

To stay in touch connect with him on LinkedIn:
www.linkedin.com/in/devmodi

Foreword

Being a member of the British Paralympic Swimming Team for 17 years was an incredible experience. Of course, it was an honour to represent my country, travel the world and win medals. However, what had a greater impact on me was witnessing how truly diverse teams can achieve greatness when inclusive environments are created.

Whilst there may still be some who question the prominence of inclusion and diversity agendas within organisations, the vast majority of business leaders understand that a diverse workforce and an inclusive culture drive business performance. The very fact that you are reading this foreword would indicate that you are yourself inclusive, or at least aspire to be. You are the future of business leadership.

However, as noble as it is to aim to create inclusive environments and leaders, without clarity on how that can be achieved, it is unlikely to happen. As Peter Drucker once said 'Do not measure yourself by your goals but by what you are doing to achieve them.'

As well as laying out the business case and the broader benefits of an inclusive society, the Inclusive Leader Scorecard clarifies how individuals and organisations can measure themselves as they strive to unlock business performance through inclusivity. The author's knowledge and passion for the subject shines through and this practical guide will have a significant impact on individuals and organisations alike.

— Marc Woods

Former British swimmer, who competed at five Paralympic Games. In his 17 years of competition he won 12 Paralympic medals, including four gold medals, from five Paralympic Games held in Seoul, Barcelona, Atlanta, Sydney and Athens.

Introduction

During the year 2020, everything I had learned and practiced would be tested. As we experienced the most dramatic shift in the world of work in my lifetime, I felt a personal responsibility to be a part of the solution. I decided during the Covid-19 lockdown to start writing this book as I felt leaders, whether they worked for a corporate, government agency or an NGO, had a critical part to play in ensuring we come out of the crisis more inclusive than before, rather than more fragmented, polarised and insular. The urgency of this book became even more apparent to me as I observed senior business icons across the globe flounder, freeze and have knee-jerk reactions to the BLM movement in the USA, UK and the rest of the world. I realised our leaders were ill-equipped to navigate us through the storm.

In a world marked by accelerated change, the fabric of our society, communities and families are being tested and transformed as never before. Unfortunately, chaos and ambiguity in the workplace and market are creating high levels of stress, pressure, disconnection, isolation, loneliness and fear. Competition is intense, and sometimes it can be vicious and unforgiving. This has required business leaders to evolve and adapt at speed, but their biggest challenge has been to find support and guidance that works in the real world.

This book is a pragmatic guide which makes inclusion strategies and concepts accessible for business leaders. I have utilised my experiences working as a chartered organisational psychologist with thousands of leaders across global brands over the last 20 years to extract the essence of what inclusive leadership really means. My understanding has been informed by transformational work I have delivered for traditional organisations such as BP and Deloitte to those at the forefront of technological change such as eBay and PayPal. These insights assemble around a model I have termed the 'Inclusive Leader Scorecard', designed to help leaders focus on the four quadrants of self, team, culture and brand.

I strongly believe that leaders have a vital role to play in influencing and revolutionising the world we live and work in and fill the vacuum created by people losing trust in traditional centres of authority. A new breed of leadership is required to navigate forward by helping us to feel a sense of belonging and allowing us to embrace the diverse uniqueness of what it means to be human. Inclusive leaders who enable diversity to flourish are vital in today's environment. Just as whole industries are being disrupted by new business models, it's time for a radical shift in leadership behaviours, attitudes and mindset. What is needed is a radical upgrade of inclusive leadership—something which is fundamentally disruptive.

This book is written for the business leader who is interested in leading from the frontlines, not simply delegating the inclusion and diversity (I&D) agenda to human resources or a passionate minority group. A leader who really understands that people are the most valuable asset in a business and is therefore prepared to invest the time and money required to unlock the power of diversity. In other words, a leader who walks the talk.

My central purpose is to 'enable a more inclusive world, one leader at a time'. With this mantra, in my heart and mind, I look forward to taking you on a journey to unlock the power of diversity in your organisation and beyond.

> *Be strong enough to stand alone, smart enough to know when you need help and brave enough to ask for it.*
> — Anonymous

Chapter One

Enabling an Inclusive Society

Understanding Our Wiring

People are usually afraid of change because they fear the unknown.
But the single greatest constant of history is that everything changes.
— Yuval Noah Harari, *Homo Deus: A History of Tomorrow*

The focus I hear too often is on survival of the fittest as the cornerstone to our evolution, taken from Darwin's *Origin of Species* (1859). However, in the 828-page sequel, *Descent of Man* (1871), which focuses on how human society can progress, Darwin refers to 'survival of the fittest' twice but mentions love 95 times. He comments on selfishness 12 times, but 92 times on moral sensitivity, competition 9 times and 24 times on mutuality and mutual aid. What the word-counts allude to is that Darwin believed empathy, cooperation and inclusion are key to our progress as a species.

The sense of wanting to be included is a basic human need that has been present since humans first lived in small societies. Belonging to a group was how you survived and protected yourself against neighbouring tribes that may attack you or try to steal your food. This sense of belonging was balanced with a need for uniqueness, awareness of your individual role and recognition for your special contribution within the tribe. This sense of social cohesion and togetherness provided the physical safety required for individuals to move beyond fear to exploration, discovery and growth.

In recent times the traditional support structures, such as the nuclear or extended family, are disappearing and in the vacuum individuals are increasingly looking to the organisation for a sense of inclusion—their colleagues have become their new 'tribe'. However, with economic uncertainty comes the threat of having to move on from job to job and role to role, bringing in its wake the disappearance of former friendships and connections. This has resulted in a lot of pressure to create a sense of belonging and connectedness that is challenged by modern day working practices, especially given the predominance in virtual working. Now your tribe might include colleagues on the other side of the world who you have never met, leading to a huge push towards digital collaboration and working together with two-dimensional pixel representations on a screen rather than human faces in the flesh. This requires leaders to constantly evolve how they create and build inclusion with their teams. Standing still even for a moment can mean you are left behind in the fast current of technological progress.

The Fourth Industrial Revolution

The pace of our learning now needs to be greater than the pace of change for us to succeed. As a global society we've travelled relatively slowly through three past industrial revolutions, but we are progressing through the fourth revolution at warp speed as we enter sci-fi reality. The changes are so profound that from the perspective of human history there has never been a time of greater promise or potential peril (Klaus Schwab, 2016).

› First industrial revolution: The revolution of mechanisation, steam power and weaving loom.

› Second industrial revolution: The revolution of mass production, assembly line and electricity.

> Third industrial revolution: The revolution of automation, electronics and IT systems.

Now we are collectively progressing through the fourth industrial revolution—the revolution of cyber-physical systems, smart robotics, artificial intelligence, quantum computing, and the internet of things. According to a Bloomberg and United Nations environment report in 2018, a growing global economy and population will lead to an increase in the world's energy demand by 30% by 2040. This revolution will force entire industries to re-think processes, competitiveness and accountability. Consider how quickly traditional industries are being turned upside down by new business models; Airbnb owns no property and Uber owns no cars. The speed of change will be phenomenal as industry and society hyper-adapt.

No industry will be left unscathed by the upcoming technological changes, and if progress is not guided, the gap between the have and have nots will widen tremendously. This is why it's well past time for the conversation surrounding I&D to begin and it's well past the time to question the organisational processes we've taken for granted. This agenda has never been more important for business success. We need more inclusive leaders to enable diverse voices to be a part of the transformation and not be left behind.

The Fourth Industrial Revolution represents a fundamental change in the way we live, work and relate to one another. These advances are merging the physical, digital and biological worlds in ways that create both huge promise and potential peril. The speed, breadth and depth of this revolution is forcing us to rethink how countries develop, how organisations create value and even what it means to be human.
— Weforum.org

As we develop and come to terms with our changing work environments which are increasingly virtual, we will be faced with new problems and new challenges. As Steve Jobs, CEO of Apple, said, 'Innovation has nothing to do with how many R&D dollars you have… it's not about money. It's about the people you have, how you're led and how much you get it.'

A Rigged Game of Monopoly

Imagine you are playing a game of Monopoly with another person, but it has been rigged in your favour. You have double the money, collect twice the salary when you pass go and get to roll both dice not just one, so you travel around the board much faster and therefore have far more opportunities to buy the best real estate.

A key question to ask yourself is, 'How does being a privileged player in a game that is rigged change the way you think, feel and behave?' Psychologist and assistant professor, Paul Piff, (2015) asked this very question during his research at UC Berkeley. He and his team brought more than 100 pairs of strangers to the campus lab to play a game of Monopoly. By flipping a coin randomly, they assigned one person to have an unfair advantage and watched the game develop with hidden cameras over 15 minutes.

What they observed was surprising, to say the least. The richer player began moving their piece around the board more loudly and displayed both verbal and non-verbal signs of dominance and power. They generally became ruder to the poorer player and showboated their success. The most shocking fact was at the end of the game, when the richer player was asked why they thought they had won, they didn't talk about the advantages they began with but talked about how they had made the right decisions and earned their success.

This experiment provides a metaphor for understanding how people view advantage in the real world. Dr Piff and his colleagues have found across multiple studies, that as individual wealth increases, levels of compassion and empathy reduce and feelings of self-interest and deservingness increase. But there is light at the end of the tunnel. In the research they found that subtle nudges reminding people of the benefits of cooperation, giving and sharing, encouraged wealthier individuals to be more pro-social and be just as egalitarian as those with less. Those in organisational positions of privilege, by becoming aware of the advantages they have, can make a decision to support those they lead, especially individuals facing greater barriers to success due to socio-economic, biological and historic factors, to name a few. The acknowledgment by leaders of inequities that exist in society and the commitment to take tangible action sets a firm base from which to build a more inclusive organisation.

Inclusive Capitalism

To ensure the fourth industrial revolution is a force for good and not destruction and meets our inherent needs as human beings to belong and contribute, leaders need to consider the concept of inclusive capitalism. How does the overarching business strategy of your organisation balance producing economic benefit with creating an inclusive society? How central to your purpose statement is the idea of inclusion? How often do your leaders, whether they are the CEO or front-line employees, speak with passion and pride about the impact your company is having on making a positive contribution to the communities you serve?

As part of my research for an executive leadership session I was designing, I discovered Nigel Wilson, the CEO of Legal & General, is a vocal proponent of inclusive capitalism. He believes that decades of unrestrained capitalism have created inequities in society that have widened and left many frustrated with an unfair system which has left so many behind. To address this, he has been a driving force in ensuring the business strategy of Legal & General is based on inclusive capitalism and is backed by action including wielding their power in the FTSE100 by investing more in companies that can tangibly demonstrate progress in this area.

The following quote by Nigel Wilson (2019), summarises how Legal & General are using their financial muscle to make a difference:

'The approach advocates for using capital to engender conditions in which people can create their own success. This is essential if we are to create a fairer society that empowers people and enables all boats to rise. With true leadership, I believe we can get there.'

What is the Vision, Mission and Purpose of your Organisation?

So, the real question this is all leading to is how committed are you and your organisation to making inclusion a reality and not just a good idea? What part does inclusion play in your vision, purpose, and mission? How does your business strategy support building an inclusive society? What tangible resources, investment and time have been allocated to making this a reality?

I believe doing nothing is no longer an option. Society is at a crossroads and leaders have a moral obligation to lead the way. Not only does this make common sense but also business sense too.

KEY POINTS

- **A sense of wanting to be included is a basic human need.**

- **As we enter the Fourth Industrial Revolution, traditional support systems disappear and opportunities to design a better way forward surface.**

- **Leaders should embrace the concept of inclusive capitalism as a force for good.**

- **A strong and inclusive vision, mission and purpose is vital for your organisation's success.**

Chapter Two

Understanding the Business Case

Pick up most mainstream publications, such as the Financial Times, Harvard Business Review or Wall Street Journal, or listen to the latest CEO announcements from the world's biggest brands and you will hear a common argument being made: organisations should reflect the diversity of the customers they serve in a global market. This is not only a moral case but is also backed up by commercial sense. What is puzzling is despite the business case being strong, progress in terms of representation is slow, especially at the top of house. I believe business leaders would make more impact if they stopped trying to justify the I&D agenda with return on investment or stock price movement and instead embraced it because it is the right thing to do.

What I have noticed is much of the evidence fails to study the part inclusion plays in unlocking the potential of diversity. To attract diverse talent you need a brand that stands for inclusion. For example, during the BLM protests in the USA and UK, many corporates made official statements regarding their stance on inclusion and diversity. Some were applauded but others were seen as hypocrites. Many of these organisations during the Covid-19 crisis had cut I&D budgets, made I&D leaders redundant and had little proof of making any significant investment in reducing inequities in society.

Once you have attracted diverse talent, they will only thrive if there is a strong inclusive culture and team in place to enable this. Ultimately, leadership is the essential building block to ensure diversity flourishes. Without an inclusive leader at the core, the entire business case for diversity quickly falls apart. And why would this happen? Because diverse talent become disengaged in an environment that doesn't live up to its glossy website or false promises during the interview process and ultimately leave.

It is still important to be aware of the research, as data drives decision making. It is also true to say that unless an organisation can embrace inclusive capitalism as a moral imperative, the commercial angle will still be the key driving force of progress. In 2020, McKinsey & Company produced the Diversity Wins Report, their findings underpinned by the largest data set to date of 15 countries and more than 1000 large companies. The data demonstrated that the business case for I&D is solid.

The relationship between increased diversity at the executive table and enhanced financial outperformance is even stronger than previously known. Companies in the top quarter for racial/ethnic diversity are 36% more likely to surpass peers, while those in the same bracket for gender diversity are 25% more likely to do the same, and this has increased from previous reports produced in 2014 and 2017. The report provided additional validation of the importance of inclusion to unlock the potential of diversity as measured through a review of employee sentiment in public online reviews. They concluded unequivocally that companies need to give greater priority to inclusion, even in industries that are considered diverse.

Additional research from leading organisations and academic institutions provides further backing to the argument, including the following:

› **Business growth.** There is a 38% increase in revenue from new products and services from organisations with diverse management teams. (The Boston Consulting Group, 2017)

› **Profit margins.** Economic profit margins increase by 30% for companies recognised for leadership inclusion. (Harvard Business Review, 2018)

› **Annual returns.** Venture capital firms that increased their female hires by 10% saw a spike in overall annual fund returns. (Harvard Business Review, 2018). Higher representation of women in C-suite level positions results in 34% greater returns to shareholders. (Fast Company, 2015)

› **Innovation.** Companies that reported above-average diversity on their management teams also reported innovation revenue (45% of total revenue) that was 19 percentage points higher than that of companies with below-average leadership diversity (26% of total revenue). (Boston Consulting Group, 2018)

› **Employee attraction.** When considering their future employment, 67% of jobseekers say that diversity is important. (Glassdoor, 2018)

› **Customer acquisition.** There is an increase of 150% customer acquisition when teams have a member of an identity group related to a segment of their target market. (Harvard Business Review, 2013)

Unlocking the Business Benefits of Diversity

Diverse organisations make better decisions, are more innovative, resonate with customers better and return more shareholder value. But there is a caveat, greater diversity does not automatically lead to better results. A study by the Canadian researcher N. J. Adler (2010), has revealed that while diverse teams do indeed outperform and out-innovate homogenous teams, they can also be significantly less effective unless led well.

Initially, diverse and heterogenous teams can actually slow things down as there is more dissent, disagreement and debate. This can make it a riskier alternative to having a homogenous group where people think and act in a similar way; enabling these teams to make faster decisions and initially become more efficient. This is the case with the private equity industry, where they hire individuals who are almost exclusively from the top business schools in the world and often similar socio-economic background. They have little impetus to change as the homogenous teams they have continue to deliver commercial success. Why change something if it is working?

Most leaders understand that cognitive diversity gives a competitive advantage. As depicted in Figure 1 from *Rebel Ideas* by Matthew Syed (2020). The rectangle represents the problem space. In box 1, homogeneity leads to little diversity of thinking and missed opportunities for innovation. Random cognitive diversity (box 2), without a strategy does little to help and can be a nightmare to manage. Curated cognitive diversity (box 3) leads to maximum impact in terms of bias being challenged and the full spectrum of intellectual power being applied to solve the problem; although much slower, it yields the best results. However, in my experience, cognitive diversity is being used as an excuse by a number of organisations as the main focus, ignoring the fact that the key variables that provide cognitive diversity are the other variables of diversity that inform and influence cognitive style.

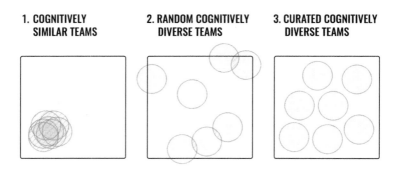

1. COGNITIVELY SIMILAR TEAMS   **2. RANDOM COGNITIVELY DIVERSE TEAMS**   **3. CURATED COGNITIVELY DIVERSE TEAMS**

Figure 1. Curated cognitively diverse teams (Adapted from *Rebel Ideas*, 2020).

A key to unlocking the commercial benefits of a diverse team is inclusive leadership. It is much easier to manage a group of people with similar backgrounds and experiences than it is to convince teams made up of diverse individuals to understand their varying thought patterns and behaviours and value them at a deep and personal level. Even when diverse teams are managed by skilled inclusive leaders, they may be outperformed by homogenous teams in the early stages because of the disruption and conflict that can result when different perspectives, experiences, backgrounds, thinking and communication styles are brought into a team. Given time, however, a well-managed diverse team can significantly outperform a well-managed homogenous one. The key is having a leader who has the mindset, behaviours and will to making inclusion a core part of their ethos rather than an afterthought.

Investing Time, Money and Energy

I'm going to suggest that creating sustainable change in the I&D space takes far more investment and time than has been historically provided. Although many organisations and their leaders may pay lip service to the idea of I&D, they fail to follow through in terms of hard graft, application and leading from the front.

Unfortunately, to get quick results, some organisations are resorting to forcing in diversity through quotas and providing financial reward for hitting them, which reinforces the very behaviours contrary to this agenda. I know this from experience, having worked at the BBC as an organisational psychologist in 2008 and being asked nicely by one hiring manager, 'Can you please just change the assessment ratings as I really need to hit my diversity quota?' My answer was a categorical, 'No', but it did make me think carefully about this issue and how having goals can backfire by driving the wrong culture.

Tokenism and doing what 'looks good' has become the norm in some organisations; it may even be the case in your organisation if you're not careful. This runs contrary to everything I stand for as a practitioner in this space. Therefore, the importance of under-standing the outcomes and impact you want as an organisation are far more important than tokenistic metrics. In my work with a recent technology client, due to the BLM protests, restricted budg-ets were opened up and the push for action finally arrived. They were intent on doing a sheep dip exercise of inclusive leadership workshops to all employees. They wanted the input to be X number of workshops delivered with the output being high attendance and 10/10 happy sheets at the end.

Clearly this was not going to enable them to deliver the busi-ness benefits of inclusion. To evolve their thinking, what we did together was to establish the outcomes they wanted in terms of a) developing leadership behaviours in the business, b) improving the level and quality of team interactions and c) increasing the quality of their conversations with customers. In other words, what was the impact they wanted to have long-term on the culture, brand and commercial performance? This enabled us to shift the initial request from being about delivering a transactional series of workshops to delivering a transformational experience. The business benefits their executive team expected were realised by reframing this as a culture change initiative tied directly to business strategy and vision, rather than an 'I&D/HR initiative' or compliance/mandatory training.

Disruptive Inclusion

If we can have conversations about disruptive business models and technologies, then it stands to reason we should be able to talk about disruptive inclusion too. I think it is time for leaders to take radical and disruptive action to build a sense of belonging, acceptance and connection not previously felt in their organisa-tions or between their colleagues. Some of you may be thinking, 'How can inclusion be disruptive? Isn't inclusion a soft, gentle word about harmony?' The term 'disruptive inclusion' may sound like an oxymoron, but I am using it because I believe the traditional methods of inclusion and diversity have limited impact. We cannot expect inclusion to stay in the past and everything else to be disruptive—inclusive leaders need to raise their game and take a step forward too. It's time for leaders to take risks, be creative and invest energy to create a workplace where people are not drowning or simply surviving, but thriving. This will bring not only commercial achievement but a sense of personal fulfilment knowing that you have made a meaningful contribution to the lives of others.

The biggest challenge facing leaders is how to create growth for their organisations. The formula for that is relatively simple. To have growth, leaders need to differentiate; to differentiate, leaders need to innovate; to innovate, leaders need diversity; to activate diversity leaders need an inclusive culture—and to manage all of this, organisations need inclusive leaders.

KEY POINTS

- Business leaders would make more impact if they stopped trying to justify the I&D agenda with return on investment or stock price movement and instead embraced it because it is the right thing to do.

- Diverse organisations make better decisions, are more innovative, resonate with customers and return more shareholder value.

- Diverse teams perform better than homogenous teams, but only if they are led well.

- If we can have conversations about disruptive business models and technologies, then it stands to reason we should be able to talk about disruptive inclusion too.

- It is time for leaders to take radical and disruptive action to build a sense of belonging, acceptance and connection not previously felt in their organisations.

Chapter Three

Shared Principles and Language

In a recent virtual session for a global technology provider, I asked the question, 'What do we risk talking about I&D and what do we risk if we don't?' This enabled the group to surface the natural fears as leaders they have of saying the wrong thing or offending someone. I remember one senior white leader saying during the BLM protests, 'If I say something I will offend someone and if I don't say anything I will offend someone.' It turned out the benefits of engaging in dialogue were outweighed by the risks, leading to silence or avoidance. I have asked these questions in numerous leadership sessions over the years and across a range of industries. The answers boil down to the following:

THE RISK IF WE TALK ABOUT IT?	THE RISK IF WE DON'T?
We will offend someone.	We will get left behind.
This is a distraction from commercial focus.	Our silence will be viewed as if we don't care.
Too political, better to not sow discord.	Unconscious biases will stay in the dark.
If it ain't broke why fix it?	We can't improve policies and processes if we don't talk.
This takes away from our meritocratic culture.	The status quo continues and the system doesn't change.

MYTH	TRUTH
1. I&D is a stand-alone activity.	I&D needs to be integrated into key cultural elements such as the purpose and vision of the organisation, people strategy, leadership development and recruitment.
2. I&D is HR's responsibility.	It is owned by every single person but especially by the CEO, Board, executive team and business leaders who have a disproportionate impact on the organisation.
3. Inclusive leadership is a new concept.	Inclusive leadership = great leadership. It is not new, but simply puts a magnifying glass on certain key elements of what make a leader outstanding.
4. I have to be from a minority group to have a point of view and right to speak.	It is ironic that some I&D experts say you have to be from a minority group to have a say— this is the most exclusive and divisive comment I have heard and surprisingly often goes unchallenged. Inclusion, by definition, requires that people from all backgrounds, whether from the majority or minority, feel they can engage in the conversation and be heard.
5. Better to be silent than offend someone.	I have seen the year 2020 intensify the polarisation of society across different identities—be it political affiliation, race or gender. Rather than encourage conversation, I have seen the shutting down of debate and refusal to hear opposing views. The result is that we hold our existing unchallenged beliefs even tighter. It is therefore essential for an inclusive leader to take risks and speak up.
6. Full representation of diversity at all levels in the organisation is the main goal.	Let's be clear, increasing diversity is important but when it becomes the overarching ambition of an organisation it can become counter-productive, forcing in minority talent prematurely rather than influencing long term systemic change and building an inclusive culture and brand.

Table 1

It can be comfortable to not bother thinking about issues surrounding inclusion and diversity. After all, if it ain't broke, why fix it? But it *is* broken and here's why. Our post Covid-19 world is going to look very different to the everyday 'normal' business world we've been living in for the past few decades. We will continue to see the rise and fall of industries, widening inequities, mass unemployment, virtual working as the norm, social isolation and economic exclusion, the list goes on and on. We are teetering on the edge of massive technological advances that will fundamentally change how we see the world and how we relate to each other. The leadership of yesterday will not get us through the challenges of the coming decade. If leaders are not leading the conversation, then what role will they play instead?

Slaying the Myths and Building Principles

What stops leaders from taking action are false myths that perpetuate and get reinforced. These incorrect assumptions sometimes are so ingrained and unquestioned, they become the accepted truth. There are six myths I come across frequently that need to be challenged for inclusive leaders to succeed. (Table 1)

Once these myths are challenged, they need to be replaced by principles that provide a true north to the organisation and the leaders within it. You may call this an inclusion charter or inclusion principles which provide guidance regarding how people should behave toward each other. It is critical that leaders are involved in the co-creation of this charter with input from a range of perspectives such as junior colleagues and minority groups. Once it is finalised, it is ideal if both leaders and their teams sign up to living these principles and over time through reinforcement, they become incorporated into the cultural DNA of the business. An example of an Inclusion charter is the following:

INCLUSION CHARTER/OUR PRINCIPLES OF WORKING TOGETHER

1. We are consciously inclusive; it is not enough to be conscious of bias.

2. Inclusion is everyone's responsibility not just HR.

3. We believe each and every one of us has a voice and a right to share it.

4. Leadership is a mindset; every person can be a role model.

5. We speak out in the face of exclusion or unfairness; silence is not an option.

6. Together, we can build a culture where we feel a sense of belonging and pride.

7. We create a safe space for diverse thought to thrive.

8. Bringing your whole self to work is not just OK, but encouraged.

9. We don't have to agree with each other to accept each other.

10. .....

What would you add, delete, amend from the above so that it resonates better to your people? Who could you share this with in your team or wider organisation to evolve it further? How beneficial would it be to develop your own set of principles to guide you as a leader, team and organisation?

Building a Shared Language

To overcome the fear barrier to engaging in dialogue around I&D, it is important for inclusive leaders to be familiar with and have a good grasp of key terms used. You don't need to be an expert and know everything but know enough to be informed and have a personal understanding of what terms mean to you and for your organisational context. There is a shared language emerging in the I&D arena, but it is important to recognise that there is still disagreement regarding terminology, concepts and ideas, so definitions continue to evolve.

When I first began to explore my interest in the I&D space, my friend, an expert in the field, tried to simplify things for me. She shared with me a range of useful phrases such as 'diversity is a fact, inclusion is a choice' and 'diversity is counting your people, inclusion is making your people count'. Just when I thought you couldn't get more simplistic than this, she said, 'diversity is being invited to the party and inclusion is being asked to dance.' So, armed with these basic layperson definitions, I began my journey into this space—barely equipped, but confident in my arsenal of common sense. Not to detract from the helpfulness of these little phrases, I will share definitions below to provide more depth.

Diversity can be defined by the protected characteristics highlighted in the Equality Act 2010 (UK), which covers age, disability, gender, race, religion, sex, sexual orientation and gender reassignment. A deeper understanding of diversity as depicted by Figure 2: The Identity Iceberg, would include further characteristics, such as cognitive diversity, neurodiversity (e.g. Asperger's, ADHD, dyslexia), personality diversity (introvert, extrovert), political affiliation (left, right, centre), cultural (nationality, regional customs) and heritage (ancestry, historic roots) diversity. In summary, I refer to these different aspects of diversity as the identities we hold. Some of these are visible and others invisible; some are important and core to who we are and others are not. Some are relevant to share depending on the context and others less so in a work context. Whereas race and ethnicity can be more visible and obvious, other identities are far more intangible, leaving it to the discretion of the individual to reveal them. Leaders can understand diversity on a much deeper level by considering the multiple and varied identities they hold as well as their colleagues and peers.

The term 'intersectionality' was coined in 1989 by professor Kimberlé Crenshaw to describe how race, class, gender, and other identities 'intersect' with one another and overlap. We are complex beings with multiple identities that make up who we are. The intersection of some of these identities impact the way we are perceived and treated and in turn, influence the way individuals

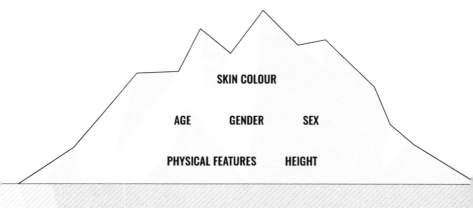

SKIN COLOUR

AGE   GENDER   SEX

PHYSICAL FEATURES   HEIGHT

SEXUAL ORIENTATION   ACCENT   CULTURE   LANGUAGES

ETHNICITY   THINKING STYLE   PERSONALITY STYLE

NEURODIVERSITY   PHYSICAL DISABILITY   MENTAL HEALTH

COGNITIVE DIVERSITY   RELIGION AND BELIEFS

SOCIO-ECONOMIC STATUS

HERITAGE   NATIONALITY

CULTURE   FAMILY STATUS

Figure 2. The Identity Iceberg

engage with the world around them. For example, the experience of a gay, Muslim woman entails a very different lived experience (the first-hand experiences one has in life) to someone who is a straight, conservative white male. Your awareness of intersectionality will enable you to have a more nuanced understanding of diversity and enhance your ability to connect to others on a deeper level.

Bringing Diversity to Life: The ICES Model

The ICES Model provides a structure for leaders and teams to engage in open dialogue around key aspects of diversity—the core identities that make up how a person views themselves. For many, providing a structure, process and framework for what may be perceived as a sensitive topic really helps to build confidence and comfort to engage in dialogue.

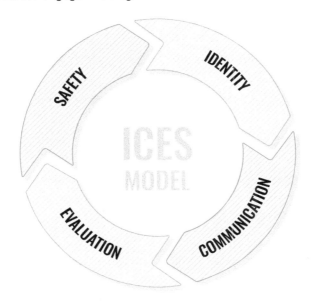

Figure 3. The ICES Model™ (Dev Modi, 2020)

> **Identity.** The most important identities we have which may be visible, less visible or invisible.

> **Communication.** How we communicate those identities (by choice or not).

> **Evaluation.** The judgements, biases and stereotypes we believe others are attributing to us, positive or negative, based on perception or reality.

> **Safety.** The degree to which I feel more or less willing (psychologically safe) to share more of myself and my identities as a consequence of these evaluations.

When I have led leadership team sessions, I have used the ICES structure as a foundational model to help participants become comfortable talking about I&D. In a workshop setting, I usually start with sharing my own reflections with the group (Figure 4.) which then sets the scene for leaders to share their personal responses with each other. The key feedback I have heard as a consequence of this exercise is, 'I have learned more about my colleague who I have worked with for 10 years in the last 5 minutes!' and 'I have noticeably felt a stronger connection with my group and greater trust as I now know more about who they are and what is important to them'. The additional impact is that leaders start to realise regardless of whether they are an upper-class, white male or a transgender Buddhist woman, that everyone has a right to engage in conversations about I&D and that the more you do it, the easier it gets and the deeper the relationships build.

As you can see from the ICES Model, diversity and inclusion are distinct concepts, but they are connected and impact each other. Historically, organisations have placed greater emphasis on diversity at the expense of inclusion—this is ill-advised. You may attract/fool diverse talent to join your organisation due to carefully curated websites and brochures but without an inclusive culture

IDENTITY	COMMUNICATION	EVALUATION	SAFETY
British Indian (visible) Born in Harrow, London. Indian parents who were refugees from East Africa due to the fall of the British Empire.	I communicate this due to my skin colour and Indian name.	+ Must be good at maths, which is actually true! – He is not one of us, not good at sport, eats only curry...	I am very proud of my British Indian identity, but when growing up I struggled due to the negative evaluations made.
Vegan (less visible) People only know this about me if I choose to share it or we first go out for a meal.	I state this verbally only when required as part of a team/client lunch or dinner meet up.	+ A healthy choice, tell me more. – You must be malnourished, you are really missing out!	I feel very safe now to share this identity but in my early career I was the outlier amongst colleagues and felt like an imposition.
Religion (invisible) I am spiritual but usually this is not relevant to share in the workplace and nothing about me would give this away.	No one know this about me unless I reveal it and it rarely comes up in conversation.	+ Someone who is driven by a higher meaning – A New Age Hippie type	Although I rarely share this in the workplace, when I meet colleagues or clients who are open about this I feel a deeper level of connection and permission to share too.

Figure 4. Reflections using the ICES Model

that supports diversity, talent quickly sees through this and leaves, doing more damage than good. Therefore, inclusion is the foundation to enable diversity to flourish. It is not an either/or equation, they go hand in hand.

Inclusive Leadership

Before defining inclusive leadership it is important to first understand what we mean by inclusion. A definition of inclusion that resonates for me is '...the degree to which an employee perceives that he or she is an esteemed member of the work group through experiencing treatment that satisfies his or her needs for belongingness and uniqueness.' (*Journal of Management*, Vol. 37 No. 4, July 2011). The relationship between belongingness and uniqueness from an inclusion viewpoint is illustrated in Figure 5. Simply put, belonging is the need to form and maintain strong and stable interpersonal relationships, the result being that individuals seek out other people similar to themselves in order to feel accepted and included, you could say being part of an in-group. At the same time, individuals need to feel a sense of individuality and be recognised for their unique contribution, a separate and distinctive identity from the group identity. Individuals try to balance these two needs through an optimal level of inclusion in the groups to which they belong (*Optimal Distinctive Theory*, Brewer, 1991). If an individual's sense of belongingness and uniqueness is put in danger, the theory suggests these individuals will do everything to try and put it right.

It follows logically based on The Inclusion Framework, that an inclusive leader is the key enabler of the top righthand box—an enabler of inclusion, balancing the core human needs of belonging and uniqueness for those they work with and lead in their teams, organisation and customers too. A brand that meets these needs truly differentiates and moves from being viewed as a commodity to becoming an icon in the marketplace.

My leadership definition which pulls together the various concepts discussed so far and underpins the scorecard framework is: 'Inclusive leaders create the conditions in their organisation and in society for inclusion to flourish and diverse individuals to thrive.'

This book unpacks the mindsets, beliefs and behaviours that enable inclusive leaders to fulfil this definition. As you go through each chapter and understand the Inclusive Leader Scorecard, you will be exposed to tools, tips and case studies to enable you to make a sustainable impact.

	LOW BELONGINGNESS	**HIGH BELONGINGNESS**
HIGH VALUE IN UNIQUENESS	**Differentiation** Individual is not treated as an organisational insider but their unique characteristics are seen as valuable and required for the group's success.	**Inclusion** Individual is treated as an organisational insider and encouraged to retain and express uniqueness in the team.
LOW VALUE IN UNIQUENESS	**Exclusion** Individual is not treated as an organisational insider with unique value to the team.	**Assimilation** Individual is treated as an organisational insider but only if they conform to the dominant cultural norms and downplay uniqueness.

Figure 5. Inclusion Framework (Adapted from Shore et al, 2011)

KEY POINTS

- There are risks to not addressing what I&D means within the workplace.

- It is important for leaders to build a shared language and embrace open dialogue in the I&D space.

- An inclusion charter provides a set of shared behavioural principles individuals can commit to role modelling.

- Inclusive leaders create the conditions for inclusion to flourish and diverse individuals to thrive in the organisation.

Chapter Four

Journey from 'Ignore it' to 'Evolve it'

One day Alice came to a fork in the road and saw
a Cheshire cat in a tree. 'Which road do I take?' she asked.
'Where do you want to go?' was his response. 'I don't know,'
Alice answered. 'Then,' said the cat, 'it doesn't matter.'

— Lewis Carroll, *Alice in Wonderland*

As with any journey, it is important to know where you are starting, where you need to go and how far you need to travel. It is useful along the way to have landmarks to ensure you are moving in the right direction. I believe having a map of progress for your I&D journey is essential, but it is important to recognise the path can be unclear and non-linear. It can feel like you are taking two steps back before taking a step forward, especially given the world around us is changing faster than we can sometimes keep up.

In the I&D Maturity Model (Figure 6), there are five overarching stages of progress from 'Ignore it' to 'Evolve it'. As a leader, team or culture moves through these stages, both engagement and the level of progress across the organisation increases. Given the impact of Covid-19 and the BLM movement, some of my clients who thought they were ahead of the competition such as at the stages 'Believe it/Live it', have subsequently realised they are actually lacking in tangible action and have been criticised by media pundits and employees for being asleep and at times blocking change, the 'Ignore it' stage. This has impacted their brands and how they are viewed in the market. More than ever consumers have been voting with their feet, comments and clicks.

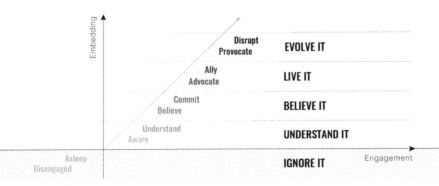

Figure 6. The I&D Maturity Model™, Dev Modi (2020)

Leaders must pay attention to the space between where they are currently standing on the maturity model and where they want to be over a given timeframe. Consider the following questions to help you:

› Where would you place yourself on the I&D Maturity Model today versus where you realistically expect to be over the next 12 months?

› Where would you put your organisation, is it ahead of your personal journey or behind?

› What will it take for you to bridge the gap and what will it take for your organisation to do the same?

› What power and influence do you have to help your organi- sation progress?

To read more about each of the 1–10 steps look at the descriptions in Figure 7, which will help you to understand what they mean and inform your personal and organisational assessment.

Mind the Gap: The Disconnect Between Inclusion and Diversity

As you plot your way forward on the I&D maturity model, you may notice there is a disconnect between what you believe and what others in your organisation perceive in terms of progress along the curve. The Accenture 2020 equality report says that two thirds of leaders (68%) feel they have created empowering environments within which their employees can be authentic, raise concerns that trouble them and innovate without fear of failure. But when the employees themselves were asked, just one third (36%) agreed. Of more importance is the fact that while leaders think an inclusive culture is important, most of them are not prioritising it. Only 21% identified culture as their top priority and only 23% had set a related goal. They discovered that within organisations that had consciously inclusive leaders, i.e. aware, active and engaged leaders, that sales and profits were measurably higher. Unfortunately, only 6% of the leaders in the survey (rising to 9% of women leaders) reached the standard of inclusive leadership.

So, if you understand that inclusion and diversity are a pre-requisite to excellence and you recognise potential gaps, what is your responsibility moving forward? Quite simply to role model inclusive leadership, enable inclusive teams around you, grow an inclusive culture and deliver an inclusive brand. The following chapters will look more closely at each individual quadrant of the Inclusive Leader Scorecard and identify the specific dimensions that are critical to your success.

KEY STAGE	IMPACT	CATCHPHRASE	STEP	DESCRIPTION
Ignore it	Destructive	**I&D is a waste of time/not necessary.**	1. Disengaged	Actively disinterested and blocks progress at every step.
			2. Asleep	Oblivious to the topic and the impact on the business or brand.
Understand it	Reactive	**I&D has to be done so we do it.**	3. Aware	Open to learning and finding out more as it seems like the right thing to do.
			4. Understand	Curious and makes an effort to intellectually understand the core concepts and issues.
Believe it	Aspirational	**I&D is important to success.**	5. Believe	Emotionally connects with the topic and has a strong conviction in the benefits.
			6. Commit	Makes tangible commitments to action that are critical to progress.
Live it	Pragmatic	**I&D is part of everything we do.**	7. Advocate	Actively talks about, promotes and rallies people behind the cause.
			8. Ally	Proactively reaches out to support those who are disadvantaged and create opportunities.
Evolve it	Innovative	**I&D is critical to our business strategy, vision and purpose.**	9. Provocate	Challenges the ways things are done and is unrelenting both internally and externally.
			10. Disrupt	Creatively reinvents the way things are done that takes the industry in a bold new direction.

Figure 7. The I&D Maturity Model descriptions, Dev Modi (2020)

KEY POINTS

- The I&D Maturity Model allows leaders to track their current state-of-play and progress of their organisations within the I&D space.

- There are five stages of progress from 'Ignore it' to 'Evolve it'.

- Leaders may recognise a disconnect between their personal perceptions of progress versus the views of others in the organisation.

- Leaders have a personal responsibility to develop along the continuum and take the wider organisation with them.

Chapter Five

The Inclusive Leader Scorecard

The key question I hear from leaders is, 'I am being asked to be inclusive and to help my team and the organisation, but I don't know what I am supposed to do and how to do it?' When I reviewed the latest research and existing resources available, I could not find a holistic model that provided leaders with a pragmatic and impactful way to develop themselves. I embarked on analysing the latest research, industry reports and models as part of a thorough literature review. I then utilised 1000s of leadership assessments and inclusive leadership workshops I had delivered over the years and extracted the key patterns and insights. I consolidated my understanding and experiences into a framework and received feedback from I&D industry experts to ensure it hit the mark. After further finetuning, I developed the Inclusive Leader Scorecard. This is a diagnostic framework for leaders which focuses on the four key quadrants of self, team, culture and brand which are further segmented to provide a total of 12 dimensions that lead to excellence in inclusive leadership.

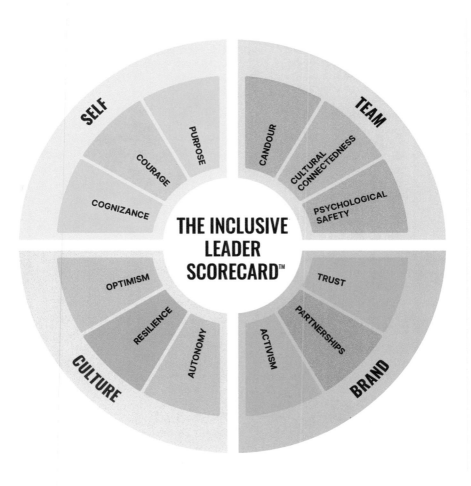

Figure 8. The Inclusive Leader Scorecard, Dev Modi (2020)

LEADING SELF
How do I model inclusive leadership?

Purpose
I act with a deep-seated drive to build an inclusive workplace and society.

Cognizance
I bring awareness and inquisitiveness to how I think and what I believe about myself and the world.

Courage
I act with self-assurance, vulnerability and confidence to challenge the status quo and take risks.

LEADING TEAM
How do I enable my team to be inclusive?

Candour
I create a team where we can be forthright, open and caring.

Cultural connectedness
I enable individuals to understand and connect with the diverse cultural identities represented in the team.

Psychological safety
I build a team where individuals can bring their whole selves to work without fear of judgement.

LEADING CULTURE
How do I grow an inclusive culture?

Optimism
I build a culture of hope and confidence in the organisation.

Resilience
I enable a culture of adaptability and responsiveness to change.

Autonomy
I promote a culture of ownership and self-direction.

LEADING BRAND
How do I deliver an inclusive brand?

Trust
I help to build trust in the brand and what it stands for in the eyes of diverse stakeholders.

Partnerships
I build relationships with diverse external networks that enhance the brand.

Activism
I support the brand in driving societal impact that has lasting results.

Leading Self: How Do I Model Inclusive Leadership?

'Start with why' is a popular phrase in leadership development, which emphasises the first step for leaders to focus on is understanding their personal *purpose*. It is important to consider what your purpose is beyond external drivers such as status, security and power and instead consider intrinsic motivators such as contribution, competence and meaning. In particular, how do these align with inclusion? To uncover and be aware of one's intrinsic drivers requires you to be *cognizant*. In addition, this self-awareness needs to be applied to what internally blocks you from achieving your purpose—such as mind traps and biases that have a detrimental impact on inclusion. Finally, *courage* is an essential ingredient, because to champion inclusion you have to speak up, show vulnerability, make mistakes and take risks to expose and express yourself and be unpopular.

Leading Team: How Do I Enable My Team to Be Inclusive?

This quadrant is a natural progression from self-leadership. Once you as the leader have reflected upon your own actions towards inclusivity, it's time to shift the attention to your team. It's your role to provide what the team needs to succeed and through the process of modelling, take your team along with you. This requires you to create an environment where candour is the norm, enabling team members to demonstrate they both care about each other personally and can challenge each other directly. You will need to enable *cultural connectedness*—an understanding of the cultural nuances of each individual based on the diverse identities they bring to the team. The previous two dimensions are made possible by creating an environment of *psychological safety*, where all team members feel safe and able to be authentic and bring their best selves to work without fear of reprimand or judgement. Research by Google's *Project Aristotle* (2012) indicates that psychological safety is by far the biggest predictor of successful teams. Individuals within teams with higher levels of psychological safety are less 'likely to leave, and more likely to harness the power of diverse ideas from their teammates. They also bring in more revenue and are rated as effective twice as often by executives.'

Leading Culture: How Do I Grow an Inclusive Culture?

If a leader only focuses on self and team development, the benefits will only go so far. To have a more ambitious impact, you will need to see yourself as a culture creator rather than passive player. Organisational culture includes an organisation's expectations, experiences and philosophy, as well as the values that guide organisational behaviour. Culture is based on shared attitudes, beliefs, customs and written and unwritten rules that have been developed over time and are considered valid (The Business Dictionary). Simply stated, organisational culture is 'the way things are done around here.' (Deal & Kennedy, 2000)

As a leader, you will need to consider how to build *optimism* in the organisation, especially during bumpy global and regional challenges. A key factor will be how you galvanise the employee base to focus on opportunities and a bright future rather than the dark cloud that may be overhead. This is not about happy-clappy optimism, you will need to be realistic about the challenges and obstacles ahead. Next comes *resilience*, which is a connected concept but goes a step further. This is about how you as a leader in the organisation build the capability of the business to adapt and respond to changing circumstances with skill and sensitivity. Creating a cultural shift cannot be done alone, as a leader you will need to enable *autonomy*. This will be bolstered by building a sense of ownership and agency amongst the employee population, so that each person feels a personal sense of belonging to the organisation and what it stands for.

Leading Brand: How Do I Deliver an Inclusive Brand?

Here, you will need to look beyond the scope of the organisation and out towards external stakeholders such as customers, investors, shareholders and society. The first dimension is *trust*. As a leader how do you engage with external stakeholders, customers and social media to demonstrate that I&D is not just a buzz word but something you and your organisation care deeply about? Once you gain trust, when something does occur in the mainstream media, your organisation can speak with authenticity and evidence to back up good intentions. Trust is closely allied to reputation. Reputation is lost when trust is lost, it can take years to build and moments to destroy. Next comes *partnerships*. You will need to network and build diverse partnerships in order to broaden thinking and reframe how the organisation is viewed by others. This is connected to the idea of ensuring that as a leader of the business you partner with suppliers, stakeholders and customers in a way that demonstrates your convictions. The final dimension is *activism*. This is about how as a leader, you influence the organisation to move beyond profit and commit to making a tangible societal impact as part of organisational ambitions.

I know that to be excellent in each and every quadrant and dimension is impossible, nor is it expected. What is important is for each leader to be honest with themselves and consider where their strengths, weaknesses, blind-spots and opportunities for growth are. Ideally, as you go through each chapter you will get a sense of this and at the end of each quadrant you can complete the short self-assessment to begin to build up a picture of your Inclusive Leader Scorecard.

The most effective leaders are not great at everything or average at everything, but tend to have a spikey profile. As a leader, what is important is for you to find your sweet spot that combines each of these quadrants in a way that unlocks your potential to be a disruptor and provocateur in the I&D space. Once you find your sweet spot, you can lead with authenticity and impact, and truly make a difference. The following chapters will take a more in-depth look at the four quadrants of inclusive leadership in turn, offering you a road map to building a fully inclusive and diverse organisation.

KEY POINTS

- **The Inclusive Leader Scorecard is a framework for leaders which focuses on the four key quadrants of self, team, culture and brand.**

- **Each quadrant includes three supporting dimensions, to provide a total of 12 dimensions.**

- **As a leader, focus on the key dimensions that will make the biggest difference to you and your organisation rather than aiming to be excellent on everything.**

Chapter Six

Self Quadrant: Modelling Inclusive Leadership

Whatever action is performed by a leader, others follow in their footsteps. And whatever standards they set by exemplary acts, all the world pursues.

— Bhagavad Gita 3.21.

As part of my younger years studying eastern philosophy, I came across the above quote from a conversation recorded 5000 years ago in the famous yoga text Bhagavad Gita, where Lord Krishna provided the warrior and prince Arjun guidance regarding duty, servant leadership and sacrifice. What struck me was how relevant these words were today as they were then, as they focused on the special role of leaders to demonstrate their values through standards, behaviours and actions, rather than 'virtue signaling'. I think John Wooden says it best when I paraphrase, 'be more concerned with your character than your reputation, because your character is what you really are, while your reputation is merely what others think you are...the true test of a person's character is what they do when no one is watching.' This chapter is all about answering the question, 'how do I model inclusive leadership?' and encompasses the three dimensions of purpose, cognizance and courage.

Purpose

The first dimension under the 'leading self' quadrant is purpose. In recent times there has been a revival of interest in the topic of purpose, and organisations have embraced it as a core driving principle. However, on an individual basis, many leaders still seem unclear and confused by what purpose means and how this concept can benefit them. I believe the process of understanding your purpose, articulating it and living by it, is integral to being inclusive. Your purpose represents a consolidation of your values and the contribution you want to make to the world, so it is inherently about helping those around you. When articulated in a statement, it provides you with the clarity needed to follow 'true north' and guide you during times of turbulence and change. Your purpose can be the source of courage to fight against the inequities faced in society which require a deep and unshakeable resolve to do the right thing.

Consider the fictional parable attributed to Christopher Wren. He was commissioned to build St Paul's Cathedral after the great fire of 1666. One afternoon in 1671, he observed three bricklayers working hard at various points along the construction. He asked the first bricklayer, 'What are you doing?' to which the bricklayer replied, 'I'm building a wall.' The second bricklayer said, 'I'm a bricklayer, putting money on the table for my family and retirement.' But the third and final bricklayer, said with a glint in his eye, 'I'm a cathedral builder. I'm building the greatest cathedral the world has ever seen.'

The first bricklayer has a job, the second has a career; the third has a calling based on meaningful work and purpose. In the parable, everyone has the same occupation, but their subjective experience and how they view themselves and their work could not be more different.

Your purpose is your brand—what you stand for and what drives you forward. It's not an outcome, but a direction, a compass to provide guidance to your choices. It's your big 'why' that underpins what you do and how you do it. Your underlying purpose may be articulated differently depending on who you are speaking to and the context, but the essence remains consistent. Your purpose speaks to your uniqueness, the special way in which you serve the world. Yet, it also speaks to belonging, as through your particular service you also connect and contribute to those around you. Purpose is not selfish; it extends beyond oneself and therefore builds inclusivity.

The idea of purpose is the notion that what we do matters to people other than ourselves. Human beings have evolved to seek meaning and purpose because the drive to connect with and serve others promotes our survival—people who co-operate are more likely to survive than those who don't. Society depends upon stable interpersonal relationships and our desire to connect with others is a fundamental human need.

For many, the experience of meaningful work is deeply personal. When you have a sense of purpose you feel passionate, innovative and committed; your outward-looking focus is on serving the organisation. Ideally, your professional purpose should be in balance with your personal purpose and values. By working from a place of meaning and purpose, a person is less likely to act from a place of fear or judgement thereby making better and more fulfilling decisions.

In 2016, LinkedIn wrote the largest global study on the role of purpose in the workforce. They found that professionals spend a majority of their hours awake at work and yet two out of three of them are disengaged in their jobs. Only 30% of the U.S. workforce reported being actively involved, enthusiastic and committed to their work. I can only imagine if the study was done again towards the end of 2020, the results would be even starker. There has never been a more crucial time to connect people with their purpose.

The study claims that people are increasingly looking for jobs that give them personal fulfilment and, in turn, organisations are seeing that purpose-oriented employees are more productive and successful. As the economy evolves, purpose and recruiting purpose-oriented talent will be a competitive differentiator. Organisations of all sizes and industries are realising the power of inspiring employees with a strong social mission and creating an environment that fosters purpose. This is called having a 'purpose mindset'. Leaders, such as the motivational speaker Daniel Pink, have referred to purpose as a 'mind enhancing drug' because of the expansiveness a strong sense of purpose can foster. Having a clear sense of purpose and meaning in your work are closely aligned with feelings of inclusion. When 'leading self' you may find that:

› You place a higher value on meaningful work.

› Your sense of contribution, purpose and meaning are intrinsically rewarding.

› You are a more supportive and developmental leader.

By aligning your personal purpose with your organisation's values, you should feel that your daily work contributes to a broader meaning. This enlivening sense of contribution is a direct result of purpose. The twin notions of contribution and purpose are found to be more valuable and life affirming than mere financial reward. Purpose, together with the modelling of courage and vulnerability are catalysts for personal success and happiness. Along with cognizance—the knowledge and awareness of oneself, an individual begins the journey towards mastering the practice of inclusive leadership.

CASE STUDY   **PURPOSE AND INCLUSION**

GLOBAL OIL AND GAS COMPANY

Challenge. The organisation was facing disruption, trying to cope with rapid changes in the energy sector and environmental challenges from customers. The net effect was they were ultimately failing to attract top talent. Historically, seen as a job for life, change happened slowly, and the organisation had a leadership culture that was too comfortable maintaining the status quo. A mindset shift was needed across the leadership population to better prepare them for ongoing volatility and to maximise any chances of success.

Solution. To meet the needs of the market, rapid change and disruption, the CEO and senior team committed resources to an extensive leadership programme. I co-led a project to take the top-tier of senior and mid-tier leaders (4000 globally) through a transformative programme of personal change. The programme was a three-day programme with virtual coaching, residential workshops with groups of 50 and online communities. All of this centred on key topics such as inclusion, purpose and accountability.

Impact. As part of the programme, leaders identified and articulated their purpose statement to each other and considered how this could help drive action and change in the organisation. This was by far the most transformative element of the programme. I saw leaders who had worked at the organisation for 20 years, logical and rational task focused engineers, become vulnerable and share their purpose statements with each other, including the emotional back stories. There were often very few dry eyes left in the room. The connections amongst leaders became far deeper than they could have ever imagined and the sense of inclusion was extraordinary. I remember vividly when one Latino woman who was in a group with three white men from Texas, said and I paraphrase, 'when I first sat down I dreaded the coming days as I thought to myself, what do I have in common with these individuals? But at the end of this programme, I realised how wrong I had been as I was able to connect with the human experience each of us shared. Thank you'.

ACTIVITY   **PURPOSE DISCOVERY QUESTIONS**

Grab a notebook and find a place to be free from distraction. Put on some meditative or instrumental music if it helps and take at least 90 seconds per question to freely write down your thoughts, without censor or judgement, considering both personal and professional life. Ensure you give yourself enough space and time to go through the following questions and write down your responses.

1. What energises and enthuses you the most in your life?

2. What are the most important tasks you want to accomplish personally and professionally?

3. Reflect on your life today. What's great about the way you're living it and what's not?

4. What's holding you back in life?

5. From your past, what are you most grateful for?

6. When looking back, what were your biggest failures and what did they teach you?

7. Imagine, you have one more day to live. How would you like to be remembered?

8. Think about the people who love and know you best. What are their highest hopes for your future?

9. From that future, look back at where you are now. What advice would you give yourself?

10. Write down a few sentences that best describe your values, what you stand for and the contribution you want to make in the world.

Please note: Your answer to question 10 is the rough content to refine and develop your purpose statement. Once you have crafted this, commit to sharing it with family, colleagues or your team. Your purpose and the way you articulate it is ever-evolving, so don't be surprised if it continues to change and take twists and turns over time.

Don't aim at success. The more you aim at it and make it a target, the more you are going to miss it. For success, like happiness, cannot be pursued; it must ensue, and it only does so as the unintended side effect of one's personal dedication to a cause greater than oneself or as the by-product of one's surrender to a person other than oneself. Happiness must happen, and the same holds for success: you have to let it happen by not caring about it. I want you to listen to what your conscience commands you to do and go on to carry it out to the best of your knowledge. Then you will live to see that in the long-run—in the long-run, I say!—success will follow you precisely because you had forgotten to think about it.'

— Viktor E. Frankl, *Man's Search for Meaning*

Cognizance

Over the last decade, there has been an explosion in unconscious bias training and the research has suggested that these workshops have done little to create change. Some would say the workshops actually do the reverse by giving people an excuse to not change as they can now blame bias as the culprit rather than take ownership. That is why I think it is time we moved from unconscious bias to conscious inclusion. The concept of cognizance sits at the heart of this transition. Courage and purpose require a certain level of cognizance: knowledge and awareness of oneself. We may think we know ourselves better than anyone else, but do we really? Are we aware of our personal biases and what do we do about them? Are we truly inquisitive about ourselves and adapt dynamically, or do we just accept ourselves as we are—static and unchanging?

Nobel prize winner, Daniel Kahneman (2002), designed a theory of cognition, the central thesis of which is there are two co-existing modes of thinking. He calls these 'System 1' and 'System 2': System 1 is the mind's fast, automatic and intuitive approach to thinking where mental activities become automated through extensive practice. System 2 is mentally slower and analytical; reason and rationality dominate.

System 1 type thinking can be a barrier to achieving inclusion. The bias that is inherent in our communities and society helps maintain the status quo because the human brain has evolved to deal with the increased complexity, diversity and constant changes that we experience by using mental shortcuts. Although we don't like to believe it—the fact is that as human beings, we are irrational. Kahneman estimates that as much as 90-99% of our thought processes, choices and behaviours occur automatically in our subconscious brain (System 1).

Although the subconscious brain evolved primarily to ensure our survival, in certain circumstances, it also holds us back from thinking objectively and being inclusive. The brain receives more than 11 million bits of information at any given moment via the total sum of our senses. To cope with this complexity, we developed generalised rules, shortcuts and assumptions about the world around us. These biases allow our thinking to happen without wasting a lot of energy on complex interpretations. Unfortunately, this can lead to errors in judgements and decisions which are not registered in the conscious mind (System 2). We are all subject to unconscious bias, but it's accompanied by the problem that bias can make us act in the opposite way to our own values and beliefs. Unfortunately, the fact that we understand bias and how it works does not reduce the impact of bias in the unconscious mind.

Personal Bias and Its Impact on I&D

Surfacing and counteracting bias and its impacts is not only the right thing to do, it's essential. In the workplace, biases can be barriers that not only prevent people from working together effectively but also damage the development of inclusive relationships that foster innovation. If your impressions of others are based on first-hand observation and actual interactions, then you are probably more objective in your thinking. However, if your impressions rest on assumptions and generalities about a group that a person belongs to, then most likely you have a biased attitude. What productive steps can be taken to change your opinions about someone who, in some way, is different from you? An important factor is to admit that you are not very familiar with the culture, values, and practices of people whose backgrounds are not the same as yours. You need to be willing to learn and develop a clearer understanding of how their experiences affect their work styles, behaviour, communications and relationships.

Biases Relevant to the Workplace

Below is a simple list of some of the main biases that affect our thinking in an organisational setting. Knowing these core concepts and examples of bias are the first step to raising cognizance levels.

› **Anchoring bias.** Over-relying on the first piece of information obtained and using it as the baseline for comparison. E.g. if the first applicant has an unusually high test score, you might set the bar so high that applicants with normal scores seem less qualified than they otherwise would.

› **Availability bias.** A singular memorable event places an undue impact on future decision making. E.g. Jack is discounted for a promotion as he is harshly marked down for an early mistake in his career which although small went internally viral and now is etched in your mind.

› **Confirmation bias.** Paying more attention to information that reinforces previously held beliefs and ignoring evidence to the contrary. E.g. you believe women are more intelligent and selectively focus on aspects of resumes that highlight the intelligence of female applicants.

› **Fundamental attribution error.** Overemphasising personal factors and under-estimating situational factors when explaining other people's behaviour. E.g. if an employee is late, you conclude he is irresponsible or lazy, rather than consider other explanations such as a traffic incident.

› **Halo and horn effect.** Having an unrealistic positive or negative lens through which a person is viewed that colours subsequent experience of them.

› **Social comparison bias.** You have a feeling of dislike or competitiveness towards someone seen as better than oneself and actively stop them from progressing. E.g. hiring a mediocre performer into the team so that your own position is not threatened even at the expense of the organisation.

› **Zero-risk bias.** Preferring the choice that provides certainty of a smaller benefit as opposed to an alternative with more risk and greater potential benefit. E.g. a candidate who is the safe bet as they are similar to existing individuals in the team rather than the person who brings something different.

› **Affinity bias.** You favour people who are more like you, i.e. they look, sound and behave similarly to you. With affinity bias you tend to ignore faults in people who are more like you and notice faults in people who are less like you.

› **Stereotyping.** You generalise behaviour to an individual based on a collective assumption about a group they belong to. E.g. you hired candidates successfully from a particular academic background and now have the stereotype that all candidates with these credentials will provide the same results.

› **Groupthink.** This occurs when you are a member of a group of well-intentioned people who make irrational or non-optimal decisions due to the power of conformity and consensus and the discouragement of dissent.

ACTIVITY   **THE COGNIZANCE PROCESS**™

You can use the following 5 steps to move from unconscious bias to conscious inclusion by asking yourself the following questions:

IDENTIFY BIAS	UNDERSTAND THE ORIGIN	CHALLENGE AND REPLACE	RAISE COGNIZANCE	BE CONSCIOUSLY INCLUSIVE

Identify bias

> Name the key biases you have e.g. assumptions, judgments and stereotypes you have about yourself and others.

> How strongly do you hold on to these beliefs?

Understand the origin

> What are these key biases based on? I.e. evidence from the past versus perception?

> When have these biases helped you or hindered you?

Challenge and replace

> Which biases have led you to exclude or treat others unfairly?

> What new beliefs can you replace the bias with that are more inclusive?

Raise cognizance

> Having become more aware of your biases, how do you feel about them now?

> What does this teach you about yourself and the type of leader you want to be?

Be consciously inclusive

> What tangible actions can you take as a consequence of this exercise?

> What experiences, individuals and ideas do you need to engage with to become more inclusive?

Self-reflection

The important thing is not to stop questioning. Curiosity has its own reason for existence. One cannot help but be in awe when he contemplates the mysteries of eternity, of life, of the marvellous structure of reality. It is enough if one tries merely to comprehend a little of this mystery each day.
— Albert Einstein

Cognizance at its simplest is about self-reflection, taking the time to think about, meditate on, evaluate and give serious thought to your behaviours and motivations. It's the process of being inquisitive and pitching deeply into your thoughts, emotions and motivations and determining the *Why*? behind them.

Self-reflection allows you to:

> Gain perspective.
> Respond more effectively.
> Learn and understand more deeply.

Self-reflection is about analysing your thinking processes from both a macro and micro level. At a macro level, you can evaluate the overall path of your working life—you can see where you're headed, determine whether you're happy with the direction and make adjustments as necessary. At a micro level, you can evaluate your responses to particular circumstances and events. Pay attention to micro behaviours, subtle behaviours that happen on a day to day basis in every interaction that either build inclusion or chip away at it one word, expression and gesture at a time. Reflection is a deeper form of learning that allows you to retain aspects of any experience, be it personal or professional: why something took place, what the impact was, whether it should happen again—as opposed to just remembering that it happened. It's about clarifying your thinking and identifying what really matters to you.

ACTIVITY   **BUILDING COGNIZANCE THROUGH FEEDBACK**

As an inclusive leader, it's necessary to not only accept feedback, but to encourage it from those around you. By using a 360 degree feedback process or simply using email, you can obtain feedback from direct reports, peers and senior stakeholders to understand your strengths, developmental areas and blind-spots. I recently facilitated a team coaching programme where I used a framework called Johari's window with senior leaders after they had individually completed a 360 degree feedback process on each other.

After completing a 360 degree feedback process, here are the steps I went through with the senior leadership team which you can try for yourself:

1. Draw on a blank piece of paper a 2 by 2 grid as depicted in the diagram below but without the text in each of the boxes.

2. Write down as much detail as you can in Box 3, which represents what is known to you, but not to others.

3. Incorporating feedback you have obtained from the 360 degree process populate Box 1 and Box 2, ensuring you balance strength and development areas.

4. Box 4 represents your untapped potential which is unknown and emerges as you become more cognizant. This can be used as a space to capture new hypotheses about yourself that are untested but important to consider.

5. Take a step back and reflect on the depth of your answers. How easy did you find that? Where are the gaps in your knowledge? How well do you know yourself? Who else can you ask for feedback to help you?

6. In an act of courage and vulnerability, who can you share your Johari's Window with? This can be an opportunity to build trust and to express how people may have misunderstood you. You can ask your team questions in an open forum where there may be areas of confusion or disagreement in terms of how you are perceived (of course not mentioning any names and maintaining confidentiality). This exercise has the potential to be profound both individually and for your team.

BUILDING COGNIZANCE THROUGH FEEDBACK

What I know
about myself

What I don't know
about myself

What others
know about me

1. OPEN AREA

What a person knows
about themselves and
is known by others in
the group or team.

2. BLIND SPOT

What a person does
not know about
themselves but which
others know.

What others don't
know about me

3. MASK

What a person
knows about
themselves but
others do not know.

4. POTENTIAL

What is unknown
by the person about
themselves and is
unknown by others.

The Johari Window

Courage

> *Courage is a heart word. The root of the word courage is cor—*
> *the Latin word for heart. In one of its earliest forms, the word*
> *courage meant, 'To speak one's mind by telling all one's heart.'*
> *Over time, this definition has changed and today, we typically*
> *associate courage with heroic and brave deeds. But in my opinion,*
> *this definition fails to recognise the inner strength and level of*
> *commitment required for us to actually speak honestly and openly*
> *about who we are and about our experiences—good and bad.*
> *Speaking from our hearts is what I think of as 'ordinary courage'.*
> — Brene Brown

Being courageous requires you to take interpersonal risks and demonstrate a level of vulnerability. Professor and author, Brene Brown (2015) suggests there is a widely accepted myth about vulnerability—that it's a form of weakness. 'But vulnerability is the core of all emotions and feelings. To feel is to be vulnerable.' If you wish to create an atmosphere where people can belong, contribute and thrive, the work starts at home—with you. A leader needs courage to act in accordance with their own convictions and purpose, especially if personal risk-taking feels uncomfortable.

As a leader you have a responsibility to be a role model of inclusive behaviours, allowing yourself to learn from others and letting go of any preconceived biases you may have. It can be hard to let go of the idea you are right and it takes courage to own your own limitations, but organisations that make measurable progress in the areas of I&D often do so thanks to advocates who lead by example. Championing inclusion requires the courage to speak up and say if you think things need to be done better or things need to change. It requires that you speak up when you see others being ignored and becoming comfortable with uncomfortable conversations. Courage is about taking risks to challenge aspects of yourself, others and even systems which you perceive create exclusion.

Role Modelling Courage

You can't be a spectator of courage, it is not a theoretical concept, but active. It requires leaders to step into the arena and be proactive rather than waiting for someone else to. As Theodore Roosevelt says so eloquently here,

> 'The credit belongs to the [person] who is actually in the arena, whose face is marred by dust and sweat and blood; who strives valiantly; who errs, who comes short again and again, because there is no effort without error and shortcoming; but who does actually strive to do the deeds, who knows great enthusiasms, the great devotions; who spends himself in a worthy cause; who at best knows in the end the triumph of high achievement, if he fails, at least fails while daring greatly...'

In the fast paced world we live in, it is so easy to get goal obsessed and focus on the future without considering the history and the lessons that have shaped you as a leader.

In early 2020, I delivered a culture change programme for a global e-commerce company focused on inclusive leadership, but with a particular focus on courage. During the first part of the leadership session, the Head of the UK business shared his 'lifeline' in front of his team of 40 senior colleagues. It was one of the most emotional moments we had experienced as his stories brought laughter and tears over a 10 minute presentation. The leader shared a picture of his life-line showing two separate lines which each represented his life from birth to the present time in relation to personal and professional life respectively (Figure 9.). The leader tracked the moments in his life that made an impression or a difference—good or bad, negative or positive. The personal and professional lines enabled him to identify how these aspects to his life experience had converged and diverged at various critical points. The high and low points in the graph and the stories behind them provided us with a clear indication of the values he lived for.

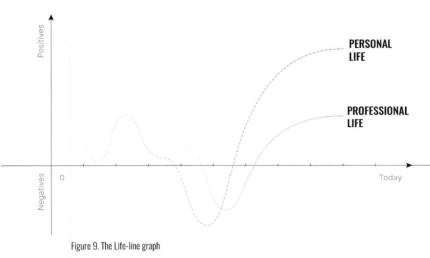

Figure 9. The Life-line graph

By putting himself in a position of vulnerability and going first, he gave others permission to do the same.

I've seen professional and personal life-lines tracking each other, and I've seen life-lines go in the opposite direction to each other—there are no right or wrong life-lines. Sometimes, someone might be having a great time at work, but their personal life is going through a rocky patch and it's work that's actually helping them through and giving them something to focus on and I have seen the same in the opposite direction. The idea is for leaders to ask themselves what they stand for as they experience these varying ups and downs in their lives? What are the necessary values and meanings that underpin their actions and behaviours, thoughts and feelings? During this exercise, I also asked the leader to think about who their personal courageous role models were/are, and whether they model themselves on them in any way? Also, what individual decisions did they make to pivot in a new direction? As this particular workshop was inclusion related, I asked the leader to consider when he felt included in his life and when he felt excluded? If he had professed he'd never felt excluded, I would have asked him to talk to those who have to build his own understanding and empathy.

As a consequence of the workshop, the levels of trust in the team skyrocketed, enabling them to have more open and honest conversations with one another. They also launched their engagement survey during the first week of lockdown in the UK and amazingly their results had gone up by 15%; this was a surprise given they had flatlined for three years prior. This further proved that courage in action can be transformative and lead to tangible business benefit even during a crisis.

> *Without courage we cannot practice any other virtue with consistency. We can't be kind, true, merciful, generous, or honest. I've learned that people will forget what you said, people will forget what you did, but people will never forget how you made them feel. If you're always trying to be normal you will never know how amazing you can be.*
> —Maya Angelou

ACTIVITY   **YOUR LIFE-LINE GRAPH**

1. Get a blank piece of paper or do this digitally.

2. Draw out the X and Y axis.

3. Go as far back into your life as is helpful, which may mean you begin during your formative early experiences and stop the graph when it hits the present day.

4. Draw one line to represent the ups and downs in your personal life, and as you age in the graph bring in a separate line to represent your professional life, ideally using a different colour.

5. Consider the following questions:

   • What are the personal and professional choices you have made that have been turning points in your career? Can you describe the shift?

   • What conflicting priorities do you need to manage at work and in your personal life?

   • What helps you feel happy and successful, personally and professionally?

   • What would you like to start, stop and continue?

6. Who can you share this with? For example, your coach, mentor or colleague? Are you able to present it to your team as part of a wider trust building exercise?

INCLUSIVE LEADER SCORECARD   **SELF ASSESSMENT**

Take a look at the Self Quadrant and rate on a scale of 1–10 how well you are doing along the three dimensions of PURPOSE, COGNIZANCE and COURAGE.

| 1 > 2 > 3 > 4 > 5 > 6 > 7 > 8 > 9 > 10 |
| significant development area > development area > moderate > strength > outstanding strength |

KEY POINTS

- The three supporting dimensions of the Self Quadrant are purpose, cognizance and courage.

- Your purpose is what you stand for and what drives you.

- Cognizance refers to the knowledge and awareness you have of yourself.

- Courage requires you to take interpersonal risks and demonstrate a level of vulnerability. A leader needs courage to act in accordance with their own convictions and purpose, especially if personal risk-taking feels uncomfortable.

- Asking for and receiving feedback is a key strategy to raise personal awareness.

- Looking back on your life can provide insights that can enable you to become a better leader in the future.

Chapter Seven

Team Quadrant: Enabling an Inclusive Team

Teamwork is the ability to work together toward a common vision. The ability to direct individual accomplishments toward organisational objectives. It is the fuel that allows common people to attain uncommon results.

— Andrew Carnegie

The second quadrant of the Inclusive Leader Scorecard moves from self to team. Enabling an inclusive team is served by the three dimensions of: *candour, cultural connectedness* and *psychological safety* and seeks to answer the question 'how do I enable my team to be inclusive?' Professor Leigh Thompson of the Kellogg School of Management defines a team as 'a group of people who are inter-dependent with respect to information, resources, knowledge and skills and who seek to combine their efforts to achieve a common goal.' Teams normally have members with complementary skills who coordinate their efforts to allow each member to maximise their strengths and minimise their weaknesses.

Developing an effective team can take considerable time and members can go through several recognisable stages before they become fully cohesive and united with common goals. Building on the content shared in Chapter 2 regarding cognitively diverse teams, Figure 10 overlays research by Katherine Phillips (2014) on homogenous versus diverse team productivity with Bruce Tuckman's (1965) *Forming, Storming, Norming and Performing* model of team maturity. The graph depicts the necessity of inclusive leadership to unlock the power of team diversity.

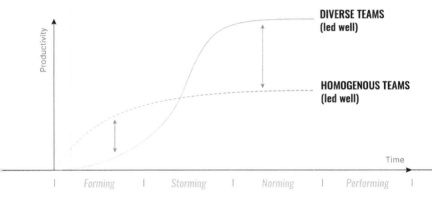

Figure 10. Leadership impact on diverse teams

> **Forming.** When a new team forms, members are polite, anxious to make a good impression and possess a strong drive towards agreement and finding commonality. Homogenous groups find this stage easier, whereas diverse teams need more time to get to know each other.

> **Storming.** Members start pushing against well-established boundaries. Disagreements and conflict are common. This is the stage where teams and the leader are most likely to fail. Homogenous teams typically experience less turbulence, due to a likelihood of 'groupthink' and other biases based on shared experience. A diverse team will have more disagreement due to a greater range of perspectives.

> **Norming.** The team with guidance from an inclusive leader move towards a place of greater trust. There is more discussion and acceptance of difference and the unique contribution of each person. The diverse team can harness differences to bring cognitive breadth to idea generation and decision making, ultimately becoming more productive.

> **Performing.** The team engage in robust dialogue with each other; there is a shared purpose and vision everyone is aligned with. The diverse team if led well continues on a trajectory of thinking in ways that are more varied and broader, leading to higher productivity.

As a team progresses through each stage, the three dimensions of candour, cultural connectedness and psychological safety determine the speed and effectiveness of the transition from forming to performing. It is also important to remember, this is not a linear model and depending on the inclusive environment created, it's expected a team will go back and forth from one stage to another.

Candour

For the purposes of this tool, I define candour as 'the ability to speak directly with empathy'. An inclusive leader is not only candid themselves, but they create an environment that enables a culture of candidness in the team. Candour enables healthy transition through the four stages of team formation and ensures once at the performing stage, a team can sustain it. As you can see in the support and challenge matrix, Figure 11, an environment of low support and challenge, is one which leads to apathy, disengagement, inertia and inefficiency. High challenge and lack of support becomes a harsh environment which is stressful and lacks empathy. Although the team may achieve amazing results it is unlikely to be sustainable and there can be a trail of disaster in the aftermath of such a leader. An environment of high support, where there is a lot of care and attention but little challenge leads to a cosy state of affairs, individuals coast along without growing. In the top right box, candour, or as Dr John Blakey (2015) calls it in his adaptation of the model, 'the loving boot', enables high performance when a leader sets this as the modus operandi, by ensuring individuals feel nurtured as well as stretched.

Figure 11. Support and Challenge Matrix (Adapted from John Blakey, 2015)

Lack of candour stems from avoiding difficult or uncomfortable conversations. There are many reasons for this avoidance, ranging from the human tendency to avoid conflict to the inherent power imbalances in organisational hierarchies that make it difficult to 'speak truth to power.' We tend to silence ourselves due to a perceived lack of credibility, or when we fail to fully grasp the facts. Sometimes we withhold our views out of genuine desire not to offend people. This was particularly evident to me during the Black Lives Matter protests that swept through America and the UK. I spoke to many senior white leaders who told me in confidence, 'I am really uncomfortable speaking my mind as I have views but feel I have no right to express them. I'm stuck, what do I do?' Ethnicity, racism and prejudice based on skin colour was something they had never experienced personally. In my conversations with them, my advice was to be authentic, listen attentively and don't be afraid to ask questions. It is easier to have a dialogue and have candid conversations if there is a foundation of care and support that has been built already.

The American business executive, Jack Welch (2006), provided three key reasons for being an advocate for candour. Firstly, you get more people into the conversation, generating better ideas and more opportunities to learn. Secondly, candour speeds up problem solving by putting issues on the table faster, thirdly, candour reduces cost because it fosters more efficient processes and helps leaders avoid costly mistakes that arise when people are afraid to speak up.

ACTIVITY   **UNDERSTANDING YOUR SUPPORT-CHALLENGE MATRIX**

To enhance your ability to be candid with your team, do the following exercise:

1. Draw a 2 by 2 box on a blank piece of paper or create it digitally.

2. Write down the names of individuals in your team and how you relate to them in terms of providing support and challenge. Please note, this is about how you relate to them rather than how they treat you.

3. What do you notice? Are there particular characteristics of the individuals in the different boxes? How do they relate to you, i.e. is the relationship reciprocal and equal, or do you notice a difference because of hierarchy?

4. What needs to shift in your relationships towards them to enable you to be more candid and create a culture of candour in the team?

5. You may want to do this exercise again but this time switch the direction, so you consider how team members respond to you. Consider how easy you make it for them to show you support and challenge you.

6. Once you have completed this exercise, who can you share the results with? Who can you partner with to explore what this means for you and your leadership of the team?

Psychological Safety

Psychological safety is being able to show and employ oneself without fear of negative consequences to self-image, status or career.
— Kahn 1990

When people talk about feeling safe at work, you imagine they are discussing their physical safety but what about their psychological safety? Do you or your team members feel safe enough to speak up and have your voices heard? Do you feel safe enough to not feel ridiculed if you speak your mind? Many organisations have a strong 'unwritten' rule not to speak up and take risks. Unfortunately, this only leads to stasis and lack of creativity and innovation. In order to increase inclusion in the team, leaders need to create a workplace that embodies 'psychological safety'. This concept overlaps with the dimensions of candour and courage but is distinct in that the focus is on creating the safety required for these behaviours to thrive.

Amy Edmondson (1999), professor of leadership and management at Harvard Business School and the most prominent academic researcher in this field, defines psychological safety as 'the shared belief among team members that the team is safe for interpersonal risk-taking'. In the simplest of terms, you feel psychologically safe in your team if you feel at ease with admitting to a mistake, pointing out a mistake made by a team member, speaking about work-related matters without censoring yourself and trying out new things.

ACTIVITY   **HOW PSYCHOLOGICALLY SAFE IS YOUR TEAM?**

Edmondson measures psychological safety across these four areas:

Attitude to risk and failure. The degree to which it is permissible to make mistakes.

Open conversation. The degree to which difficult and sensitive topics can be discussed openly.

Willingness to help. The degree to which people are willing to help each other.

Be yourself at work. The degree to which you can bring your authentic self to work and are welcomed.

In order to establish whether you as an inclusive leader are creating an environment of psychological safety for your team members, ask yourself the following questions, and if you are feeling brave, ask your team too, either in your next all hands or via a quick anonymous survey to get more honest responses:

› Do your team members feel comfortable in team meetings asking about things they do not know or understand, or do they generally try to maintain an image of perfect knowledge about work matters?

› Do your team members feel comfortable enough in team meetings to raise difficult issues, concerns and reservations about work, or about how well the team works together, or do these conversations take place informally outside team meetings?

› What happens when mistakes and critical incidents happen? Do your team members distance themselves from the issue, or are they seen as opportunities for team learning?

› How often are team members encouraged to give and receive feedback?

› Do you invite all your team members to contribute irrespective of their rank or job title?

› Do you value and utilise the skills and talents of your team members? Do you encourage them to contribute in ways they feel able to? Or do you expect them to stay within the parameters of their roles?

> › Do your team members ever feel their contributions and efforts are compromised by others in the team?

> › Do your team members ask each other and the team for help when they need it?

> › Do your team members feel comfortable expressing disagreement and offering dissenting views? Do team meetings include discussions and debates about work matters?

> › How much do you know of your team members as people outside of work?

> › How happy are you with your team's performance and your place within it?

The Business Case for Psychological Safety

Research by Travis, Shaffer, and Thorpe-Moscon (2019), from the think tank Catalyst, found evidence 'that inclusive leadership behaviours were key to creating a climate of psychological safety which, in turn, cultivated the right conditions to create high-performing teams characterised by inclusion and innovation.'

There is a clear case for fostering and cultivating psychological safety, wellbeing and job satisfaction for the team. There is also a strong business case for promoting and cultivating psychological safety in work. One popular study that makes the business case for psychological safety amongst its more than 100,000 employees is Google's extensive two-year research programme, *Project Aristotle* (2016). Google's people analytics suggested that psychological safety was the aspect most reliably shared by high performing teams and that psychological safety is strongly associated with objective (e.g. sales revenue) and subjective indicators of team performance (e.g. ratings of team performance by team members and managers, customer satisfaction with team products). The strongest effect of psychological safety on team performance appears to be:

> the beneficial effects on team learning and the faster adoption of new technologies (process innovation).

> the faster adaptation to new market circumstances and customer requirements.

> the early identification of potential risks.

> the faster development of innovative products.

In inclusive teams which are, by definition, psychologically safe, members express mutual respect, trust and interest in each other as people while arguments are decoupled from the personality of the person expressing them. Team members feel free to express themselves, ask questions, seek feedback, ask for help, critically scrutinise, raise difficult issues, concerns and problems and propose 'off the wall' ideas. They can do these things without feeling the threats of being negatively labelled, blamed, embarrassed or punished. Ultimately, psychologically safe teams encourage the expression of dissenting views on work matters and harness their internal diversity and difference.

ACTIVITY   **HOW AS A LEADER YOU CAN FOSTER
                                   PSYCHOLOGICAL SAFETY IN YOUR TEAMS**

› **Demonstrate engagement** by being present at all times and focusing on the conversation at hand. Show your interest by being interactive. Use positive verbal messages like, 'tell me more' and non-verbal active listening skills, like nodding in agreement. Be aware of your body language and practice the SOLER position (sit straight, open posture, lean forward, make eye contact and relax) to show you are making a connection and actively listening. Trying to multi-task such as writing emails when engaging in a virtual session will be obvious to others, so best to avoid it.

› **Show understanding** by recapping what has already been said and then acknowledging areas of agreement or disagreement. Be open to taking questions from within the group. Be sure to validate any comments verbally by saying things like, 'I understand,' or 'I see where this is heading.'

› **Be inclusive in the interpersonal arena** by sharing information about your own working style and encourage your team members to do the same. Try to be available to your team members and encourage conversations and feedback sessions. Say, 'thank you' to your team and to individuals when a job is well done. Step in and take control if you feel a team member is treating another unfairly. Build rapport by talking about other things apart from work with your team.

› **Make sure your decision-making is inclusive** by asking for feedback, input and opinions from your team. Try not to interrupt or allow others to interrupt—make sure everyone is heard. Explain your reasoning behind any decisions you've made by walking your team through them and highlight when other team members have made contributions to your decisions.

› **Remain confident and flexible** by managing team discussions and making sure that any conflicts do not become personal. Invite team members to challenge your perspective, to probe and push back. Model vulnerability by sharing your perspective and any work failures with your team. Finally, encourage your team to take risks and step outside their comfort zones, whilst doing so yourself.

Cultural Connectedness

Culture makes people understand each other better. And if they understand each other better in their soul, it is easier to overcome the economic and political barriers. But first they have to understand that their neighbour is, in the end, just like them, with the same problems, the same questions.

— Paulo Coelho

Cultural connectedness is about understanding the cultural identities of others and building a deeper connection based on that. It's about taking the time to relate to the 'lived experience' of a team member, not just from a place of curiosity but from a genuine thirst to walk a mile in their shoes. Cultural connectedness focuses on enabling deeper associations based on mutual respect and understanding for another's culture.

As a leader, it is necessary to have not just second-hand knowledge of other cultures, but to dive in first-hand. For example, Nelson Mandela was tuned in to the needs of not just black South Africans but also to other cultures, such as the Afrikaans. I remember watching the movie *Invictus*, which retold how Mandela's uncanny ability to connect with people from different backgrounds enabled him to utilise the Springboks to unite the country. An example of when corporates can get this badly wrong due to lack of cultural connectedness was when Gucci had to withdraw their $890 balaclava sweater in 2019 due to being widely criticised for being an example of blackface. Here was a vivid example of cultural blindness at play; not one person in the organisation thought this might be insensitive and if they did they certainly failed to speak up, or were silenced.

In the LinkedIn article, *We all speak English, don't we?*, Nannette Ripmeester (Figure 12), a Dutch author and expert in Labour mobility, humorously describes how even when we have the same language, cultural differences can mean the same phrases carry different meaning. Many of you may be able to relate to the following extract from her article:

WHAT THE BRITISH SAY	WHAT THE BRITISH MEAN	WHAT THE DUTCH UNDERSTAND
That is an original point of view	You must be crazy	They like the idea
I'll bear it in mind	I won't do anything about it	He will use it when appropriate
Could we consider some other options	I don't like your idea	He is still in the process of thinking
I would suggest	Do it as I want you to	An open suggestion
Perhaps you could give this some more thought	Don't do it, it's a bad idea	Consider possible road blocks
I am a bit disappointed that	I am very upset and angry that	It doesn't really matter
Quite good	A bit disappointing	Quite good
Not bad	(very) good	Average or poor
Please consider	Do it or forget it	He leaves it up to me
The idea described is rather original	Bullshit	It's a good idea
A few issues that need to be addressed	A whole lot needs to be changed	2-3 issues need rewriting

Where 'he' is mentioned 'she' can also be read

Figure 12. What the British Say (Adapted from Nannette Ripmeester, 2020)

'It took a while before I fully understood the British concept of phrases such as *very interesting indeed.* I once tried to use the *very interesting* in an international meeting: my Dutch and German colleagues looked at me as if I had gone nuts—thinking the suggestion was not *interesting* at all and the Australians were puzzled, the Canadians doubted my intentions and only the Brits got my underlying cynicism. So, I now stick to the Dutch directness if I want to get my point across—often introduced by the comment, "sorry I'm Dutch, so this may come across as a little direct…"'

She further provides an analysis of what the Brits say and how this is interpreted by the Dutch to bring home the point—cultural nuance matters if we want to be understood, and simply saying the same words doesn't mean we are speaking the same language.

The cultural challenges for leaders have increased given globalisation and predominantly virtual working. Leaders are working with team members they rarely meet and sometimes have never met face to face, but are required to build rapport, a sense of unity and cohesion. A helpful guide is Erin Meyer's book *The Culture Map* (2016) which decodes how people think, lead and get things done across cultures. Meyer's Culture Map provides a field-tested model for decoding and successfully leading in complex cultural environments. The culture map divides cultural habits into eight categories and then places each culture on the map to highlight the extent to which they differ (Figure 13. provides a visual depiction of how to compare and contrast different countries along the dimensions). This approach comes with a warning, don't use it to stereotype individuals. The map is intended to provide insights and hypotheses but these must be tested person by person without making generalised assumptions.

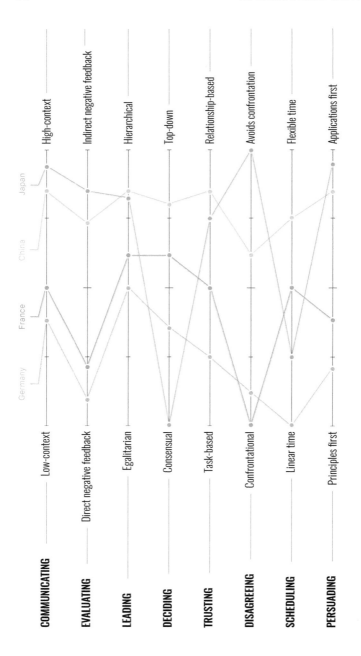

Figure 13. The Culture Map (Erin Meyer, 2016)

Communicating: Low vs. High Context

According to Meyer, work meetings in Japan can take a long time and a common assumption is that communication can be vague and take time to get to the point. What may seem as talking around the issue from a North American point of view, is called High Context Communication. High context cultures consider more details before coming to a conclusion. Meyer suggests that low-context cultures are more matter of fact in their communications and that when working with others from high-context cultures it's important to read between the lines and to reflect on what is both being said and unsaid.

Evaluating: Direct vs. Indirect Negative Feedback

Meyer suggests that in most northern European cultures, direct feedback is common, accepted and encouraged. In most Asian cultures it is unacceptable and often considered insulting. In either cultural context, using the wrong strategy can leave employees feeling demotivated and not supported. The aim is to be careful about feedback; be sure to research the culture in order not to give offence.

Leading: Egalitarian vs. Hierarchical

Comparing hierarchical and egalitarian leadership comes down to the power distance between a boss and a subordinate. Organisations in an egalitarian world, such as Australia or Scandinavia, usually have flat organisational structures where the distance between boss and subordinate is low. But in Asian or Arabic hierarchical cultures, the distance between the two is high.

Deciding: Consensual vs Top-down

According to Meyer, decision-making impacts every part of business strategy. In certain cultures, such as Japan, Sweden or the Netherlands, decisions are made in groups through consensual agreement. In the US, France, Thailand, Russia or China, the decision-making process is top-down and directive.

Trusting: Relationship-based vs. Task-based

Most Asian cultures are relationship-based, whereas most western cultures are task-based. In task-based cultures, Meyer suggests that 'business is business', but in relationship-based cultures, 'business is personal'. Potential business partners in the Middle East at the early stages will invite you into their homes for dinner with the family, whereas in the UK, this level of intimacy early on rarely happens.

Disagreeing: Confrontational vs. Non-Confrontational

Meyer suggests that in certain societies, open confrontation is encouraged and will not affect the relationship negatively. In fact, disagreement is often seen as a way to learn to explore more ideas. This is the case in Israel, which has one of the most confrontational styles of conversing. However, in some African and Asian cultures, confrontational disagreements can ruin the group harmony. When working in Asian countries, open confrontation should be carefully managed.

Scheduling: Linear Time vs. Flexible Time

In the Middle East and India, time is seen as flexible and the approach to schedules and deadlines is fluid, changing frequently as challenges and situations arise. In linear-time cultures, project steps are organised in a sequential fashion, think of the engineering perfection of German manufacturers. To many people from linear-time cultures, flexible-time cultures can appear chaotic and frustrating and conversely, linear time cultures can be viewed as stiff and constrained.

Persuading: Principles First vs Applications First

This focuses on how differing cultures convey ideas. The UK, Canada, US and Australia have an applications-first culture. This means that when making a presentation, a leader will start with presenting conclusions and recommendations before methodology. However, in Germany it's normal for a leader to lay out the theory, concepts and methodology before sharing their conclusions.

In summary, consider how well you know your team along the above dimensions, regardless of where they come from in terms of ethnicity, culture, or heritage. In today's global world, individuals are a complex blend of multiple influences such as the cultural norms of the country where they have spent most of their working life intertwined with the culture of the organisation they work for (e.g. the culture at Apple may be more dominant than the national culture of origin) and their own personal idiosyncrasies. The essential point here is not to make an assumption about someone based on their place of birth, but to get curious about their style and way of working so that you can better connect with them.

ACTIVITY   **GETTING TO KNOW YOUR TEAM ON A**
                           DEEPER CULTURAL LEVEL

As a team leader, to deepen your understanding of the cultural nuances of your team and to build deeper connections, you can try the following exercise which works well virtually, or face to face. Before the next team meeting ask each person to bring one object that best represents their cultural identity and be ready to tell a 90-second story about it to the rest of the team. Ensure everyone is in agreement regarding confidentiality and only share what they are comfortable.

A simple structure for the session could be as follows:

1. Share your object and tell a 90-second story of what it is, why you chose it and what it means to you.

2. Share appreciation as a group by thanking the person and reflecting back what you have learned about them based on the story.

3. Ask questions of curiosity to probe further to understand the cultural context of the individual.

4. You may want to use the 8 dimensions of the culture map as described to better understand each other.

INCLUSIVE LEADER SCORECARD   **SELF ASSESSMENT**

Take a look at the Team Quadrant and rate on a scale of 1-10 how well you are doing along the 3 dimensions of CANDOUR, CULTURAL CONNECTEDNESS and PSYCHOLOGICAL SAFETY.

1 > 2 > 3 > 4 > 5 > 6 > 7 > 8 > 9 > 10

significant development area > development area > moderate > strength > outstanding strength

KEY POINTS

- The Team Quadrant is served by the three dimensions of candour, cultural connectedness and psychological safety.

- Candour refers to the leader's ability to speak directly with empathy. This enables high performance by ensuring team members feel nurtured and stretched.

- Psychological safety is being able to show and employ oneself without fear of negative consequences. Leaders need to create a workplace that embodies psychological safety in order to claim to have an inclusive culture.

- There is a clear case for psychological safety in teams for member's well-being and job satisfaction, as well as a strong business and moral case.

- Cultural connectedness is about the leader's understanding of the cultural identities of others and building deeper connections, even more important given the increase of virtual working globally.

Chapter Eight

Culture Quadrant: Growing an Inclusive Culture

The world is intertwined today, much more so than it is when I was coming out of school. Because of that, you really need to have a deep understanding of cultures around the world. I have learned to not just appreciate this but to celebrate it. The thing that makes the world interesting is our differences, not our similarities.

— Tim Cook, CEO of Apple

The third quadrant of the Inclusive Leader Scorecard moves from team to culture. Growing an inclusive culture is served by the three dimensions of: optimism, resilience and autonomy. All the dimensions that were referenced under the previous quadrants are just as relevant here, particularly cultural connectedness from the team quadrant. To influence and impact the wider organisational culture requires additional strengths to all that has been described so far. The essential message for leaders to explore in this quadrant is, 'how do I grow an inclusive culture?'. Business leaders are vital to organisational culture and they must appreciate their role in maintaining and evolving it.

What is an Inclusive Culture?

Culture can be described as the system of values, beliefs and behaviours that underpin how work gets accomplished—'the way things work around here'. Whereas engagement refers to the level of commitment and fulfilment an employee gets from their work—'how people feel about the way things work around here.' (Deal and Kennedy, 1982)

It's important to remember that organisational culture is not stagnant, but fluid. Members of an organisation develop a shared belief around 'what looks right' as they interact over time. When those beliefs and assumptions lead to less than successful results, the culture must evolve for the organisation to stay relevant. Changing organisational culture is never easy. External events such as Covid-19, BLM, climate change or political unrest can apply external pressure to an organisation to review the culture they have and inclusivity of the workforce.

The Culture Web (Figure 14) is a framework used to map the culture of an organisation. It illustrates a way of seeing and understanding the different influences that affect organisational culture and can be used to represent both existing and future culture. At the core are the three principles of organisational purpose, vision and values which need to be underpinned by an inclusive ethos. This central circle is the psychological underpinning for the rest of the organisation to align with and focus on. The web of circles depicts how the constellation of stories, brand and symbols, routines and rituals, talent, organisational structures and leadership/power structures impact the culture. The interlocking circles further emphasise the dynamic nature of culture and the very reason why it is so hard to change as it can feel intangible and difficult to quantify.

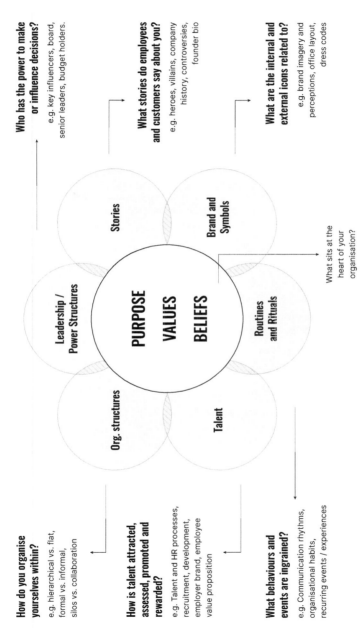

Who has the power to make or influence decisions?

e.g. key influencers, board, senior leaders, budget holders.

What stories do employees and customers say about you?

e.g. heroes, villains, company history, controversies, founder bio

What are the internal and external icons related to?

e.g. brand imagery and perceptions, office layout, dress codes

Stories

Brand and Symbols

Leadership / Power Structures

PURPOSE VALUES BELIEFS

Routines and Rituals

Org. structures

Talent

What sits at the heart of your organisation?

How do you organise yourselves within?

e.g. hierarchical vs. flat, formal vs. informal, silos vs. collaboration

How is talent attracted, assessed, promoted and rewarded?

e.g. Talent and HR processes, recruitment, development, employer brand, employee value proposition

What behaviours and events are ingrained?

e.g. Communication rhythms, organisational habits, recurring events / experiences

Figure 14. The Culture Web (Adapted from Johnson and Scholes, 2011)

ACTIVITY   **UNDERSTANDING YOUR OWN CULTURE WEB**

Draw your organisation's culture web based on your perceptions. Think about the impact of I&D on these variables and the impact of these variables on I&D. For example, how does I&D impact the way in which you attract talent to the organisation versus how does your method of attracting talent impact I&D?

With the picture of your current cultural web complete ('current state'), try repeating the process, thinking about the culture that you want ('future state'). Starting from your organisation's strategy, think about how you want the ideal organisational culture to look. Can you see what can be improved, changed and adapted? What elements of I&D would you improve in your own organisation if you could?

Consider:

> What strengths have been highlighted by your analysis of the current culture?

> What factors are hindering your strategy or are misaligned with one another?

> What factors are detrimental to the health and productivity of your workplace?

> What factors will you encourage and reinforce?

> Which factors do you need to change?

> What new beliefs and behaviours do you need to promote?

> How would you describe the culture you want to move towards, i.e. what is your vision?

One of the main reasons investment in I&D programmes has not yielded better results is that organisations have concentrated on increasing the proportion of people from underrepresented groups, rather than tackling the underlying culture. Those organisations seeing real progress are those that are going beyond a simple focus on numbers. They are addressing the climate and behaviours that determine whether diverse minority groups feel a sense of belonging. These organisations are not only achieving their diversity goals;

they are also seeing improvements in engagement, trust, creativity and performance across the employee base.

Leaders can use the three dimensions of optimism, resilience and autonomy to impact each of the elements of the culture web and drive change, not just at the core, but also for the petals.

> *There's no magic formula for great company culture. The key is just to treat your staff how you would like to be treated.*
> – Richard Branson, Founder, Virgin Group

Optimism

> *The genius of evolution lies in the dynamic tension between optimism and pessimism continually correcting each other.*
> — Martin E.P. Seligman

During the 1988 Seoul Olympics, swimmer Matt Biondi was feeling the pressure. He was tipped to beat Mark Spitz's record of seven gold medals won in 1972. The media frenzy beforehand was tremendous and the focus was all on Biondi. He swam the first race, 200 m freestyle and came in third. Although disappointing, he swam the second race, 100 m butterfly and won silver. Sports commentators and journalists alike were suggesting that it was most unlikely Biondi could rebound from this.

The disappointment of his first two swims did not deter him. He went on to win five gold medals. Professor Martin Seligman was not surprised by Biondi's success. Four months earlier he had uncovered, via a questionnaire, that Biondi had above average levels of optimism compared to others in his team. Nort Thornton, the team coach, was asked by Seligman during swim practice to lie to the swimmers about their time and to noticeably increase it. What Seligman found was that when Biondi was told he swam the 100 m butterfly at 51.7 sec during a swim practice, rather than his actual time of 50.2 sec, he tried even harder the 2nd time and achieved an improved time of 50.0 sec. Whereas Biondi's team-mates, who measured as pessimistic and were told similar inaccurate information, were actually slower on their 2nd go. Biondi was the type of athlete who had developed the winner's attitude of using defeat to spur him towards success.

In September, 2020, I delivered a virtual inclusive leadership programme to a team of 25 regional leaders for a tech giant. I put up on the whiteboard a simple line from left to right that said 'drowning, surviving and thriving'. I asked the participants to anonymously annotate with a star how they felt currently. To my surprise and to stunned silence from the group, half put a star under drowning and the other half under surviving. No one put a star in thriving. This was despite the organisation having the best financial performance in years. When I asked them what they could do about it, there was a sense of resignation that they just had to accept it and keep on going. Despite positive economic circumstances, the mood in the virtual room was of 'learned helplessness' (a term coined by Martin Seligman in 1967), a sense they had little control over the pressure and stress they were going through right now and the best thing was to grit their teeth and knuckle down. What was missing in the group was a sense of optimism, hope and belief that they could thrive and importantly, that they had the ability to influence this.

In his book *Learned Optimism*, Seligman (1990) states that optimism is a mindset that can be learned and has wide ranging benefits for leaders and workplace culture in terms of reduced stress, better health outcomes and higher motivation. Optimism does need to be counterbalanced with realism, otherwise you can fall prone to the 'optimism bias' (Tali Sharot, 2018) and engage in risky behaviour for example, where an individual might continue to smoke in the face of evidence as they have a delusional sense of indestructibility.

As an inclusive leader it is important to consider how you influence the culture to be optimistic; not a happy-clappy optimism which avoids bad news with heads in sand but a realistic optimism which faces up to challenges with honesty, integrity, self-belief and hope. But it can't stop there, as a leader you must consider how you can galvanise the wider organisation behind the shared purpose, vision and values of your company. This bolsters the sense of belonging individuals feel towards the organisation and helps them to accept they can each make a difference to influence this positive view of the future. To create this shift of mindset, it will often require repetition of core positive messages, authentically sharing bad news in the right way and challenging cultural elements (e.g. command and control leadership styles, reward structures that encourage bad behaviour, biased selection practices, etc.) which detract from building an inclusive workplace.

HINTS AND TIPS   **WHAT CAN YOU DO AS A LEADER TO BUILD OPTIMISM IN THE WIDER ORGANISATION?**

Reflect on the culture web and consider how you as a leader can leverage your personal optimism across the organisation. Below, I target three areas specifically and the actions you can take.

1. **Routines and rituals.** What are the organisational rhythms you can influence, such as corporate conferences and regional town halls, and take a leading role in sharing a message of hope regarding the future?

2. **Stories.** How can you identify good news stories about individuals across your workforce that exemplify your culture? How can you share these across the organisation more widely, such as posting on your corporate social media pages or intranet?

3. **Brand and symbols.** What positive impact on society is your brand recognised for externally but less so internally? How can you share this more widely amongst your peers and senior stakeholders?

Resilience

It is a law of nature we overlook, that intellectual versatility is the compensation for change, danger, and trouble. An animal perfectly in harmony with its environment is a perfect mechanism. Nature never appeals to intelligence until habit and instinct are useless. There is no intelligence where there is no change and no need of change. Only those animals partake of intelligence that have a huge variety of needs and dangers.
— H.G. Wells, *The Time Machine*

Resilience is best defined as successful adaptation to adverse circumstances (Zautra, Hall and Murray, 2010). Whereas optimism is about having a positive view of the future, resilience is the capability to not just believe and feel this but to adapt to the needs of the environment in a flexible and fluid way. According to the Stockholm Resilience Centre (2015), 'resilience is the capacity of a system, be it an individual, a city, or an economy, to deal with change and continue to develop. It is about how organisations can use shocks and disturbances like a financial crisis or climate change to spur renewal and innovative thinking.' In my personal experience, when an organisation is not resilient and under stress, this directly impacts the culture of inclusion, as individuals try to protect their patches and justify their positions, creating a toxic environment. When under pressure as leaders, teams and organisations, the ideal is to utilise 'eustress' or good stress to strive forward towards optimal performance (Figure 15), rather than being pushed over the edge to distress, or staying too calm and not responding at all.

In 2020, the Covid-19 crisis and BLM movement have required new levels of adaptation and resilience not experienced before. As the virus has travelled the world and paralysed whole swathes of the global economy, businesses in every sector have been left wondering how they will survive financially. Many have cut costs or furloughed their employees, some have gone out of business

Figure 15. Optimal performance

altogether. These measures have impacted disproportionately the most vulnerable in society and in particular minority groups who are frontline workers. Research by Black Rock (2020), the world's largest asset manager, shows that those businesses who are the most resilient and are doing the most good socially by protecting the communities and the environment on which they rely, are the ones most likely to survive post-pandemic.

Building Organisational Resilience

If personal resilience is about the capacity to recover quickly from difficulties, then as a leader it is your role to help the organisation adapt and respond to changing circumstances at an enterprise level. Today's business world is one that is turbulent and full of volatility, uncertainty, complexity and ambiguity (VUCA). Business continuity planning and disaster recovery planning have been on the agendas of leaders since the pandemic, but so few have a psychological resilience plan for the wellbeing of the people in the business. In order to succeed in this environment, organisations must be more adaptive and agile than ever before and organisations that lack resilience, that ability to bounce back after setbacks, are often stressful places to work. Stress lowers employee performance, productivity and morale and strains workplace relationships. Resilience is key to sustaining an inclusive culture and preventing people opting for survival mode and falling back on biased thinking.

A resilient organisation has four key benefits when crises hit (Figure 16). The first step is the anticipation benefit, pre-empting a threat is in motion and reacting quickly such as implementing disaster recovery plans at speed. The second is the impact benefit, as the organisation responds with agility and a level head to the chaos of the unanticipated stress (e.g. listening lounges to provide an outlet for employees to vent frustrations and identify solutions). The recovery benefit kicks in as the organisation accepts, responds

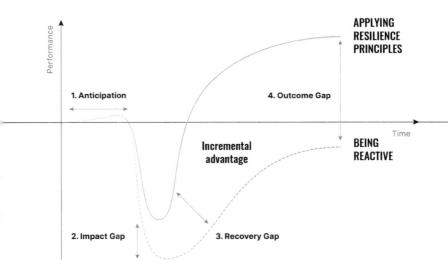

Figure 16. The Cumulative Advantage of Resilience (Adapted from Martin Reeves, HBR, 2020)

and rebounds from the crisis faster than others, putting into place new ways of working (e.g. working from home policies). Lastly, the outcome benefit enables the organisation to function at a higher level of performance due to the cumulative benefit of the previous stages (e.g. retaining best talent during the crisis, enabling growth when demand returns). You may be able to relate to these four stages given your observations of the economy and your organisation in response to Covid-19 and how, although initially most industries were overwhelmed by the immediate shock, those organisations that were most resilient recovered faster.

HINTS AND TIPS   **YOUR ROLE AS A LEADER TO BUILDING A MORE RESILIENT ORGANISATION**

1. **Be future focused.** As a leader encourage the wider organisation to take a long-term view and be strategic rather than operational or tactical. Encourage leadership to use this as an opportunity to make changes faster and quicker than before.

2. **See opportunity in adversity.** Help the organisation to step back from the chaos and to shift perspective and consider the question 'what if'.

3. **Utilise systemic thinking.** Influence senior leadership to take a step back and view the organisation as one player within a system which includes customers, investors, employees and suppliers. Without a systemic approach, any one break in the chain can cause existential threat.

4. **Reward cognitive diversity.** Identify how the organisation can recognise and reward diversity of thinking, which is essential when trying to solve new problems that have not been experienced before.

5. **Reframe change.** As Alibaba's founder Jack Ma suggests, view change as the new normal, not stability. As a leader, design the organisation to be agile, fluid and experimental.

Autonomy

The drive to direct our own lives and be the architects of our future is a psychological need that is intrinsic to who we are as humans. The motivation of your employee base is unlocked when the focus from leadership is on achieving outcomes rather than policing how they are achieved. Individuals want greater ownership, control and freedom to design a workplace that is tailored to their diverse set of circumstances. In his 2009 book, *Drive*, Daniel Pink unpacks the research and shows how autonomy is an intrinsic motivator, leading to greater engagement, fulfilment and creativity. The shift to virtual working has forced many organisations to think deeply about how to lead in a digital world. By trusting your people to follow principles rather than rules, you raise levels of trust and create a sense of belonging. Not only that, but individuals tap into their unique experiences, ideas and ways of working to add more discretionary effort and ultimately value to the business.

As leaders enable more autonomy, they need to let go of power and share it more widely. Inclusive leaders need to build a culture of confidence, where individuals are rewarded for taking responsibility and risks, but also consequently own more of the successes and failures. An inclusive leader is focused on catching people doing the right things rather than what they do wrong, listening more than telling and stepping to the side to enable others to step up.

CASE STUDY   **EMPOWERMENT AT SVENSKA HANDELSBANKEN**

An article entitled, *Harnessing Everyday Genius* by Hamel and Zanini in the Harvard Business Review (2020) states that 'This European bank treats every one of its more than 750 branches like a standalone business. Branch teams, typically eight to 10 employees, are responsible for credit decisions, loan rates, deposits, customer communications and staffing levels. In any year that the bank's return on equity exceeds the average of its peer group, one-third of the difference is put into an employee profit-sharing program that invests in the bank's stock. Each person gets an equal share of it, regardless of rank. Through the program, the employees are indirectly the bank's largest owner. Thanks largely to a well-below-average cost-income ratio, Handelsbanken has outperformed its European peers on return on equity in each of the past 48 years.'

Many leaders were unsure how to respond to the BLM protests in the USA and UK, some reached out to black employees to check in and others stayed silent for fear of saying the wrong thing. The most impactful leaders were the ones who remained open and authentic and showed concern and care for the black community, while also giving space for members of the community to voice concerns and be OK with choosing to be silent and not speak. An effective tool used by a number of organisations to empower specific minority groups was to create a safe space for them to speak and have a voice in what was termed 'listening lounges'. Individuals who were willing to speak further were given a platform to share their experiences of work and life to the board and executive team.

ACTIVITY   **SETTING UP A LISTENING LOUNGE**

Talk to as many people in your organisation as you can about the unspoken issues in your organisation that suppress feelings of inclusion. A big part of being resilient and open to change is resisting the urge to 'fix' any real or potential problems but instead taking the time to fully understand the root causes. What are some of the big challenges facing your employee base where you could build resilience by creating a space for individuals to share and be empowered?

Once you have clarity as to the purpose of bringing people together, invite the target group to a listening lounge. Ensure such an initiative is not a tick box exercise or a superficial action to show you are responding to media pressure. Instead, provide evidence of how this action is tied to a wider commitment to I&D strategy that is supported by the executive team and seen as a business imperative. This will ensure you get buy-in and commitment to the session.

During this session, be a true facilitator by asking the right questions and listening actively to the answers. In this way, you will create the space to enable dialogue and the sharing of unique experiences. With permission, share the highlights of the conversation anonymously, for the wider organisation's benefit. If possible, for those willing to share more publicly, provide a platform for these individuals to inspire the wider culture. It is these employee stories that can have the biggest potential to shift the culture.

INCLUSIVE LEADER SCORECARD   **SELF ASSESSMENT**

Take a look at the Culture Quadrant and rate on a scale of 1–10 how well you are doing along the 3 dimensions of OPTIMISM, RESILIENCE and AUTONOMY.

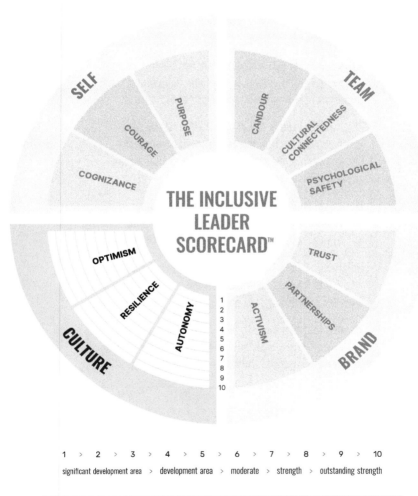

1 > 2 > 3 > 4 > 5 > 6 > 7 > 8 > 9 > 10

significant development area > development area > moderate > strength > outstanding strength

KEY POINTS

- The culture quadrant is served by the three dimensions of optimism, resilience and autonomy.

- Leaders are vital to the creation of workplace culture and they should appreciate their role in maintaining and evolving it.

- Organisational culture is fluid. It can be described as the system of values, beliefs and behaviours that underpin how work gets accomplished.

- The Culture Web is a tool to map the culture of an organisation. It illustrates a way of seeing and understanding the different influences that affect organisational culture.

- Optimism is a mindset that can be learned and which has wide ranging benefits for leaders and workplace culture in terms of reduced stress and higher motivation.

- Resilience refers to the ability of the organisation to adapt and bounce back from setbacks and your role as a leader in building this capability.

- Autonomy is the need to direct our own lives. Autonomy in the workplace is an intrinsic motivator leading to greater engagement, fulfilment and creativity.

Chapter Nine

Brand Quadrant: Delivering an Inclusive Brand

The fourth and final quadrant of the Inclusive Leader Scorecard moves from culture to brand. I think Seth Godin (2009) defines it best when he says 'A brand is the set of expectations, memories, stories and relationships that, taken together, account for a consumer's decision to choose one product or service over another.' Especially for millennials and Gen Z, the brand of choice is increasingly coming down to which organisations they believe are a force for good in society (Interbrand, 2019). As a leader you have an essential part to play to ensure your organisational brand is a positive force for change in society. Your capability to do this is served by the three dimensions of: *trust*, *partnerships* and *activism*. The essential question we will explore in this quadrant is, 'how do I deliver an inclusive brand?'.

In the wake of the George Floyd tragedy, I remember speaking to a CEO who noticed many of his competition were flocking to make public statements to show solidarity and their commitment to change, he hesitated. I remember the conversation clearly where he said with nervousness, 'I feel like a rabbit in the headlights, I want to declare our outrage and willingness to do something about inequity in society, but our past doesn't reflect this sentiment, what do I do?' I understood his hesitancy, as an organisation they had made little investment internally regarding I&D and even less externally.

He feared any communication externally would be viewed as 'opportunist' and 'jumping on the bandwagon'. After some lengthy debate and strategising, a statement was made publicly that was transparent, humble and aspirational. He stated as an organisation they had not done enough to remove inequity or support inclusion but this would change and tangible commitments were made to support a host of charities and voluntary organisations. The paradigm shift that occurred for this CEO and so many other organisations I worked with over the subsequent months signalled a sea change in the corporate world. Brands had renewed commitment to act beyond profit and make a contribution to society—and they were helped by leaders driven with a wider definition of inclusion that considered not just shareholders and customers but society too.

The 2020 Trust Barometer report by Edelman found consumer buying patterns were strongly influenced by perceptions of how actively a brand was committed to making a difference in society. They found 81% of respondents stated their buy decision was influenced by how much they trusted a brand to do the right thing. In another section, 64% chose to switch, avoid or boycott a brand based on its stand on societal issues. In relation to Covid-19, 89% of respondents stated they wanted 'brands to shift money and resources to producing products that help people meet pandemic-related challenges.' In the vacuum created by a lack of consistent and effective political response, 62% of consumers view 'brands playing a critical role in addressing the challenges we face.'

The report revealed that despite a pre-Covid strong global economy and near full employment, none of the four societal institutions measured: government, business, NGOs and media were trusted. The cause of this paradox they suggest is 'found in people's fears about the future and their role in it, which is a wakeup call for our institutions to embrace a new way of effectively building trust: balancing competence with ethical behaviour and re-training.' The Edelman Report reveals that brands face a fundamental reordering of priorities amid a global pandemic and societal outcry over systemic racism. In this environment, consumers are looking to brands to act and advocate for change and this is where inclusive leaders are required to step in.

Today, it's expected for organisations and their brands to have a point of view in order to stay relevant. It's interesting to note that Unilever brands, such as Lifebuoy and Domestos, encouraged people around the world to keep themselves and their homes as clean as possible, irrespective of whether they bought Unilever products or purchased a competing brand. The ice-cream brand, Ben & Jerry's, is another example of a brand that has been doing meaningful work towards equality and recognises that the public expects them to use their platform to speak out. It is time for brands that have not used their platform so far to be vocal about inclusion to reflect on their purpose and evaluate how they can better contribute to the conversation moving forward.

To become an inclusive brand companies must demonstrate their responsibility to society. Examples of brands responding to the current Covid-19 crisis include Pret a Manger; to show their gratitude to healthcare workers they offered all NHS staff free hot drinks and 50% off all other products. Streaming giant, Spotify, launched Covid-19 Music Relief, a global fundraising campaign to help support musicians who are having to cope with halted revenue streams. Luxury design house, Louis Vuitton used their in-house machinery for good, repurposing production lines to produce hand sanitiser and donating to key workers who would otherwise have to continue working under dangerous and compromising conditions. Deliveroo was one of the first delivery services in the UK to offer a no-contact option to help prevent the spread of coronavirus. To announce the initiative, the brand sent out a personal e-mail on behalf of founder, Will Shu, explaining the different measures they were taking to protect both their customers and their own staff. In addition, they offered customers a 10% discount for any order placed with local companies—a great way to support small businesses, customers, and the environment all in one go.

An inclusive leader sits at the nexus between the customer brand proposition and the employer brand proposition (Figure 17). They are the conduit between these two essential aspects of an organisation, not only influencing the brand people work for but also the brand people purchase. It is important to remember your people will treat your clients the way you treat your people. Consider the impact allegations of bullying had on Uber's share price and reputation and subsequent protests by drivers regarding labour rights. In the European market, these and other issues opened up space and opportunities for challenger brands to enter, such as Bolt and Kapten.

On 30 September, 2020, Glassdoor launched the 'Diversity & Inclusion Rating', which enables employees to rate how satisfied they are with inclusion and diversity at their current or former company. This rating directly impacts how brands are perceived in the marketplace, influencing customer buying decisions. As a leader, even if you do not directly influence the communication around your brand such as via the PR or marketing department, you still have an impact via the projects you deliver and how you treat employees, the suppliers you choose to work with, the LinkedIn posts you send out and the partnerships you forge with external entities such as NGOs and social enterprises.

Figure 17. Building Brand Integrity, Dev Modi (2020)

Trust

I am sure you have used an Uber at some point to travel from point A to B. A business that can build a brand that becomes a shorthand for a specific consumer behaviour is at the apex of brand building. The phrases, 'I am going to get an uber', 'let's google it' and 'shall we zoom?' are prime examples. However, due to leadership, even this cherished top of the pyramid position can wobble and be challenged. In early 2017, taxi drivers went on strike in New York City because of President Trump's travel ban, but Uber raised their prices to make more profit which then inspired the campaign #deleteUber. Soon after, Susan Fowler, an Uber engineer blogged about the discrimination and harassment she had faced from management, which subsequently led to an increased backlash. At one point it seemed that every month bore yet another PR crisis at Uber, either because of Travis Kalanick, the then CEO, or due to other leadership challenges.

When Frances Frei, Professor at Harvard Business School met with Kalanick soon after, she was expecting a difficult conversation. Instead she found him to be humble and introspective, accepting his part to play in the challenges the brand faced such as putting people into positions of leadership before they were ready or without the proper development or mentoring. She recollects in that meeting how Kalanick 'revealed a sincere desire to do the right thing as a leader.' Unfortunately, to restore trust in the Uber brand he had to step down to enable new leadership to transform brand perceptions.

Trustworthy relationships are vital to the way we do business today. In fact, the level of trust in any organisation, whether internal or external, is a strong determinant of success. The challenge is having a conceptual framework of evaluating and understanding trust. Maister, Green & Galford (2006) in their book, *The Trusted Advisor*, suggest there are four variables of trust that constitute the trust equation:

1. **Credibility.** Refers to the words we speak. For example, 'I trust her technical knowledge, any question I ask she knows what to say'.

2. **Reliability.** Refers to the actions we take. For example, 'if they said they will deliver end of the week, they will do it for sure'.

3. **Intimacy.** Refers to the safety or security we feel when entrusting someone with something. For example, 'I trust her with business-critical information, she has never broken our trust before'.

4. **Self-orientation.** Refers to the individual's focus, primarily whether the other person's focus is on him or herself, or on the other person. For example, 'I can't work with him as I feel his focus is on what he can get for himself rather than a win-win'.

Figure 18. The Trust Equation (Adapted from Maister and Galford, 2006)

The Trust Equation covers the most common meanings of trust that you may encounter in everyday business interactions. Trust whether you are an individual or organisation, requires good scores on all four variables in the Trust Equation. Volkswagen lost 'credibility' when they were identified as miscalculating CO_2 emissions, Virgin trains scored low at one point on 'reliability' for not delivering trains on time, Uber lost 'intimacy' in London when it was found that driver identity checks were sub-par and Goldman Sachs was shown to have high 'self-orientation' (leading to a lower trust score) when they were charged with selling \$1bn in sub-prime mortgage securities for a quick profit. Living the four values is the best way for leaders to increase their trustworthiness and by proactively supporting the organisation to consistently model these enables a trustworthy brand to be built. When you consider your organisational brand, how trusted is it currently and how can it maximise scores on the trust equation? What part can you play in making this shift in scores a reality?

ACTIVITY   **CALCULATE YOUR TRUST QUOTIENT**

Before you can enhance the trustworthiness of your organisation in the marketplace, it helps to understand your own score.

To calculate your TQ or Trust Equation score consider how you measure up on each element. Give yourself a score from 1–10 for credibility, reliability, and intimacy, where 10 is outstanding and 1 is poor. For self-orientation, give yourself a score of 10 if you are highly focused on your own self-interests at the expense of others, whereas 1 represents the optimal balance of consideration for others versus yourself.

Plug into the Trust equation to get a number and to convert into a % by dividing by 30 and multiplying by 100. You will notice in the formula, self-orientation has a disproportionate impact on the scores, highlighting the importance of this aspect.

Consider the same exercise as above, but now plug in the figures for your organisation's brand based on what you perceive or know from your own experience. How does the brand score compare to your score? Do you have a strength where the organisational brand has a weakness, or vice versa? What actions can you take to further build trust in your organisation?

Partnerships

At a global conference for a client, I asked attendees to complete the following exercise. As I recount the steps feel free to complete it yourself. Get a blank piece of paper, or type on a screen the 5 people you find it easiest to talk to at work. Now write down the 5 people you find it easiest to talk to in your personal life. What do you notice? What are the patterns? What characteristics do individuals share in your personal and work life? What surprises you? How consciously do you think these networks have developed, or is it by chance? How diverse are the two lists?

When I asked participants to share their answers to the above questions, the first point conveyed was many had networks which had developed organically (e.g. they grew up in a diverse area or worked in a diverse office environment), therefore diversity was present but not by conscious choice. The other observation was when individuals had the choice, e.g. the friends they made and partnerships they formed externally, they were drawn to people similar to themselves in terms of other forms of diversity such as similar social class, shared hobbies and thinking style. This linked to a concept I had studied during my early psychology training called Homophily theory. This theory formulated by Lazarfield and Merton (1953) suggests that the greatest levels of communication happen between people who consider themselves similar, allowing them a 'private language' enabling them to take short cuts in their communication process and recognise who is 'in' and who is 'out' of the group. Homophily allows us a certain level of comfort and certainty—and as such is unfortunately also an obstacle to diversity.

Homophily impacts the structure of our networks both inside and outside of work. As individuals tend to be drawn to those they feel familiar and safe with, over time this leads to exclusive networks, those who are different struggle uphill to get to the same level of rapport and depth of relationship, if ever. We've all heard the term the 'old boy's network', but what exactly is it? It's often a hard concept to explain. This usually indicates privileged, private school educated men who share opportunities among themselves and often pass this advantage on to their children. Over the course of generations this can lead to large disparities in opportunity and achievement.

So how can things change and become more inclusive? I believe as a leader you have a responsibility to take the initiative to personally build diverse partnerships outside of your organisation, that not only benefit you but also the brand you work for. Rather than this being something which is centrally driven by your PR, CSR, Marketing or HR departments, the fastest and best way for things to improve is for leaders to take personal ownership to build diverse partnerships.

There are organisations in the business world designed to enable diverse partnerships to be formed. Consider for example the organisation *MSDUK*, which is a not-for-profit organisation bringing together ethnically diverse SMEs to network with large corporates who they ordinarily would struggle to meet. Or not-for-profit organisations that are industry specific such as *WiHTL* or *The Diversity Project*, each dedicated to building diverse relationships in the hospitality, travel and leisure industry or investment and saving industry respectively. You may have professional bodies you are a member of where you can take more of a leading role to explore the I&D agenda for your specialism. You may consider becoming a non-executive director for an organisation that is making a positive social impact, enabling you to be exposed to different individuals to your existing network but also reflecting positively on the brand you work for.

Building partnerships doesn't have to just relate to connecting with organisations, it can apply to reaching out personally to individuals too. I remember reaching out on LinkedIn to Martyn Sibley from the Purple Goat Agency, who connects brands with disabled customers in the $8 trillion global disability market. I did this not only to expand my network and learn more about the unique challenges faced by those with disabilities but also to explore how this could benefit the organisational brand I worked for. I reached out to build a two-way partnership with Mark Charlesworth (mark-charlesworth.org) who is a specialist in neurodiversity, an area I felt as a brand we could utilise to be more relevant to clients from neurodiverse backgrounds. I reached out to these individuals and many more to expand my network and learning but also to be an enabler between the diverse experts I was connecting with and the brand I worked for.

ACTIVITY   **COACHING QUESTIONS TO HELP YOU FORM
                         SUSTAINABLE PARTNERSHIPS**

Get a blank piece of paper or word document and brainstorm the following:

1. Who are the potential organisations and individuals you know in your network who can provide an alternative and diverse perspective to you?

2. Which organisations or individuals will you prioritise to reach out to and take the first step towards building a more diverse set of external partnerships?

3. Why have you chosen these particular entities/people?

4. How could they benefit you and your organisation's brand, and how could you benefit them?

5. What will be your elevator pitch for reaching out – so that it is clear why you are contacting them and why it would be mutually beneficial?

6. What is your strategy past the first meeting if things go well in terms of building a long-term partnership?

7. How will you leverage these partnerships to benefit the brand you work for?

8. When will you reach out, such as a specific time and date you can set aside right now?

9. How will you measure your progress and success?

10. Who can you share your actions with so you are held to account?

Activism

More people around the world are living better lives compared to just a decade ago. More people have access to better healthcare, decent work, and education than ever before. But inequalities and climate change are threatening to undo the gains. Investment in inclusive and sustainable economies can unleash significant opportunities for shared prosperity. And the political, technological and financial solutions are within reach. But much greater leadership and rapid, unprecedented changes are needed to align these levers of change with sustainable development objectives.
— United Nations, Sustainability Development Goals (2020)

The United Nation's Sustainable Development Goals are a universal call to action to end poverty, protect the planet and improve the lives and prospects of everyone, everywhere. The 17 Goals were adopted by all UN Member States in 2015, as part of the 2030 Agenda for Sustainable Development which set out a 15-year plan to achieve the goals. Today, progress is being made in many places, but, overall, not advancing at the speed or scale required. The U.N. states that 'numerous civil society leaders and organisations have called for a super year of activism' to accelerate progress on the Sustainable Development Goals, urging world leaders to 'redouble efforts to reach the people furthest behind, support local action and innovation, strengthen data systems and institutions, rebalance the relationship between people and nature and unlock more financing for sustainable development.'

It was Peter Drucker (1946) who said (the corporation) '…is in trouble because it is seen increasingly by more and more people as deeply at odds with basic needs and basic values of society and community.' Although written almost 75 years ago, it is just as relevant today. In 2020, there has been a dramatic shift from marketing and corporate driven CSR to societal driven Brand Activism (Figure 19). Kotler & Sarkar defines this concept as business efforts to promote, impede, or direct social, political, economic, and/or environmental change with the desire to promote or impede improvements in society. In their book *Brand Activism, from Purpose to Action*, Kotler and Sarkar (2018) suggest that brands can be progressive activists—doing good in the world, or regressive activists—damaging it. Just like a knife in the hands of a criminal is deadly but in the hands of a surgeon can save a life, a brand in the hands of an inclusive leader can be a beacon of light, but led by a regressive leader, a path to societal erosion.

Marketing-driven

Cause Promotion
Cause-Related Marketing
Corporate Social Marketing

Corporate-driven

Corporate Philantropy
Workforce Volunteering
Socially Responsible Business Practices

Society-driven

BRAND ACTIVISM

Figure 19. Brand Activism (Adapted from Kotler and Sarkar, 2020)

Whereas CSR was seen as a 'nice-to-have' marketing and team-building opportunity, allowing you to take your team to the local school and paint a corridor, snap some pictures, put them on social media and then get on with the 'real business' at hand, brand activism is different. It is driven by a 'fundamental concern for the biggest and most urgent problems facing society' as Kotler & Sarkar put it. In a world more polarised than ever before, you cannot be neutral. In the past you could decide the issues you wanted to focus on as a brand, but no more. Your key stakeholders such as employees, customers, social movements and society at large decide. Brand activism is a business priority now and can make or break a business.

As a leader it is your responsibility to influence your organisation to build a brand which is progressive and has a stance and commitment to making change happen. In a Brandfog (2018) survey about CEOs and their social media activity and subsequent impact on consumer behaviour; they found 93% of respondents agree that 'when CEOs issue statements about the key social issues of our time and I agree with the sentiment, I am more likely to make a purchase from that company.' Of course, in today's world it is not just the CEO who builds the brand of the organisation, every leader does, including you.

In a survey by Ipsos, *What Worries the World* (2018), the majority of participants surveyed across 28 countries and over 20,000 interviews identified five major worries: financial/ political corruption, unemployment, poverty/social inequality, crime and violence and healthcare. Each and every one of these issues directly or indirectly impact the I&D agenda. For a brand to tackle these issues it just can't be a 'nice-to-have' but must be directly connected to business strategy as it has been for Patagonia, The Body Shop or Ben & Jerry's to name a few.

There are six key areas of brand activism as identified by Kotler and Sarkar which represent the spectrum of actions organisations are taking right now:

1. **Social activism** includes areas such as equality—gender, LGBT, race, age, etc. It also includes societal and community issues such as education, healthcare, social security, privacy, consumer protection, etc.

2. **Workplace activism** is about governance – corporate organisation, CEO pay, worker compensation, labour and union relations, supply chain management, governance, etc.

3. **Political activism** covers lobbying, privatisation, voting, voting rights, and policy (gerrymandering, campaign finance, etc.)

4. **Environmental activism** deals with conservation, ecocide, land-use, air and water pollution, emission control, environmental laws and policies.

5. **Economic activism** includes wage and tax policies that impact income inequality and redistribution of wealth.

6. **Legal activism** deals with the laws and policies that impact companies, such as tax, citizenship, and employment laws.

How can an inclusive leader make a difference and get involved? The first step is to find out if your organisation is involved in key spheres of brand activism. If the answer is yes, explore how you can get involved. If not, then take ownership and identify which one of the six areas described is best aligned to your organisation's brand and strategy and then go about influencing the key individuals in your business to make this a priority. If this cannot happen companywide, consider how in your region or function you can get the ball rolling by being a more vocal spokesperson for these issues and take a lead in your circle of power. Sometimes change happens bottom up, at the grassroots; and at other times top down, by influencing the CEO and executive team. Depending on your approach and role in the business, decide on a strategy and go for it.

CASE STUDY   **EXAMPLES OF BRAND ACTIVISM**

Axion Structural Innovations LLC is known for its commitment to sustainability. Axion builds railroad ties and pilings using recycled plastic bottles and industrial waste instead of standard materials such as wood, steel, and cement.

Ben & Jerry's is the ice cream company that made conscious capitalism central to its strategy. As stated on its website, 'Ben & Jerry's is founded on and dedicated to a sustainable corporate concept of linked prosperity.' The company supports opposing the use of recombinant bovine growth hormone and genetically modified organisms and fosters myriad values such as fair trade and climate justice.

The LEGO Group has formed partnerships with organisations like the non-governmental organisation, World Wildlife Fund. In addition, LEGO has made a commitment to reduce its carbon footprint and is working towards 100% renewable energy capacity by 2030.

Mars' 'Cocoa for Generations' is a sustainable cocoa initiative that requires its cocoa farmers to be fair trade certified to ensure they follow a code of fair treatment to those providing labour. In exchange for certification, Mars provides productivity technology and buys cocoa at premium prices.

Starbucks, which has been socially and environmentally focused since its inception in 1971, promises to hire 25,000 veterans before 2025.

INCLUSIVE LEADER SCORECARD   **SELF ASSESSMENT**

Take a look at the Brand Quadrant and rate on a scale of 1–10 how well
you are doing along the 3 dimensions of TRUST, PARTNERSHIPS and
ACTIVISM.

1 > 2 > 3 > 4 > 5 > 6 > 7 > 8 > 9 > 10

significant development area > development area > moderate > strength > outstanding strength

KEY POINTS

- A brand is the set of expectations, memories, stories and relationships that, taken together, account for a consumer's decision to choose one product or service over another.

- As a leader you have an essential part to play to ensure your organisational brand is a positive force for change in society. Your capability to do this is served by the three dimensions of: trust, partnerships and activism.

- An inclusive leader sits at the nexus between the customer brand proposition and the employer brand proposition.

- Trust relationships are vital to the way we do business today and leaders play a key role in building a brand that conveys trustworthiness to external stakeholders.

- Leaders have a responsibility to take the initiative to personally build diverse partnerships outside of their organisations, that not only benefit them but also the brand they work for.

- Leaders need to influence their organisation to take an active role in solving societal issues, choosing real world challenges their organisation is especially well placed to support.

Chapter Ten

A Toolkit for the Future

Until one is committed, there is hesitancy, the chance to draw back, always ineffectiveness. Concerning all acts of initiative and creation, there is one elementary truth the ignorance of which kills countless ideas and splendid plans: that the moment one definitely commits oneself, then providence moves too. Whatever you can do or dream you can, begin it. Boldness has genius, power and magic in it. Begin it now.
— William Hutchison Murray

To progress the I&D agenda requires every leader to make a commitment to act. Words alone cannot create the change required. Throughout this book, across each of the quadrants of the Inclusive Leader Scorecard, I have taken you through specific actions you can take to make a difference. Whereas the activities shared so far have been focused on your individual ownership, what we have spoken less about is organisational ownership. In this chapter, I walk you through tools and interventions that your organisation can consider and implement. Some of these interventions you may be able to influence directly and others indirectly depending on your role in the business. The four steps are as follows:

1. **I&D discovery audit.** Doing an in-depth review of what is happening currently in your organisation across developing leadership behaviours at all levels, building inclusive teams, growing an inclusive culture and delivering an inclusive brand.

2. **I&D vision & strategy.** Developing a vision and strategy across key areas of importance and ensuring alignment with the business and people strategy.

3. **Inclusive Leader Scorecard interventions.** Considering each element of self, team, culture and brand, designing and delivering tangible actions.

4. **I&D measurement and analytics.** Measuring key criteria so you can identify the speed of progress. You can also use the I&D maturity model to highlight organisational improvement.

Figure 20. I&D process for change

The I&D discovery audit

The I&D discovery audit if done robustly, looks at every step of the journey key stakeholders (employee, candidate, customer, supplier, etc.) go through in relation to the organisation to provide an honest view of areas of strength, development, blind spots and risk factors. The audit should be comprehensive and include the key employee segments to understand the differential impact on diverse groups. In addition, you can include the external environment, such as the way the brand is perceived and how key stakeholders (customers, investors, general public, suppliers) experience your organisation. The review utilises not just what is known to your organisation but also considers the competitor landscape in terms of differentiation.

You may not be the I&D global lead or Chief People Officer, but as a business leader you can encourage and contribute to such an audit being initiated—without it, any I&D actions will be disjointed and will be much like a scatter gun approach.

I&D Vision and Strategy

Based on the audit and recommendations, the next step to consider is developing an I&D vision and strategy. This must be aligned with the overarching people strategy and business strategy to ensure there is full buy-in. This is where you as a leader can contribute and influence the direction of thinking by getting involved. Usually you would do this in combination with a select group of business leaders, HR and the I&D lead. This is a key opportunity for you to learn, shape the agenda and have your say. The vision and strategy need to be aligned and integrated with the purpose, vision and business strategy of the organisation. The Inclusive Leader Scorecard can be used to structure thinking to ensure all elements of the workforce, workplace and marketplace are considered and fleshed out.

Interventions Based on The Inclusive Leader Scorecard

The following organisational interventions are grouped loosely around the 4 quadrants, framed in terms of providing benefit at the individual (self), team, culture and brand level.

SELF

> **Technology.** Think carefully about the technology you use in your employee processes and ensure they don't reinforce unfairness in the system. Make certain that what goes into the software does not create unintended biases, such as the

Amazon AI recruiting tool, designed to save time, that in fact provided hiring recommendations that showed bias against women and had to be scrapped.

> **Leadership development.** All leadership development initiatives need to be infused with I&D at their core, rather than delivering standalone workshops or training modules. Supporting such programmes with self-assessment questionnaires and 360 tools which measure inclusive behaviours enables focused and individualised development.

> **Line manager training.** A high proportion of individuals who leave an organisation do so because of their manager. An unhappy ex-employee can broadcast their experiences easily on social media, impacting the employer brand. Therefore, it is essential all who line manage go through regular and rigorous learning and assessment to ensure they are competent and inclusive. It is time to stop viewing line management as an extra hassle on top of the day job, but rather as critical to the day job.

> **Interview selection training.** All recruitment and interview methods should include individuals and panel members who are accredited in hiring procedures. Given the extent of human bias, it is essential that individuals are aware of personal, panel and cultural biases, so these can be mitigated.

> **Coaching.** Provide coaching for leaders to support them in how to become more inclusive as per the Inclusive Leader Scorecard. During the coaching, the leaders need to have clear goals and outcomes they want to achieve. Where possible, the line manager can be involved at the start and end of the coaching relationship to ensure the leader has their buy-in.

> **Reverse mentoring.** Diverse talent, usually from junior roles become mentors to senior leaders in terms of understanding

the I&D impact on diverse groups and what they can do as leaders to become more understanding, empathetic and active in their support.

› **Leadership assessment.** The most senior roles in the organisation should be appointed only after objective assessments have been undertaken. This is best done by an independent internal or external specialist. The use of psychometrics combined with a psychological and biographical interview can enhance the objectivity of the process. Care must be taken to adjust for specific neurodiverse conditions when conducting these assessments.

› **Onboarding.** The first 100 days in the life of a new recruit can make or break them. Given the investment and time gone into hiring the right person, it is surprising how little care is taken when onboarding key hires. Careful consideration must be paid to welcoming the individual, ensure a smooth landing and mentoring to ensure they are given the best chance of integration.

TEAM

› **Listening lounges.** Organisational listening is a useful method of understanding the perspective of wide and diverse elements of the employee base by creating a space deemed psychologically safe where people can speak their mind freely and if they wish, share their views with senior leaders.

› **ERG (employee resource groups).** These groups are usually formed around a specific minority identity group based on gender, sexual orientation, race or religion. The purpose of an ERG (also referred to as an affinity group) is usually twofold, a) to create a safe space for people to express themselves without fear of judgement and b) to educate and raise awareness in the wider organisation. If not managed well, these groups can become too insular and exclusive in nature rather than using the opportunity to have a strategic impact.

› **Team coaching.** Team coaching is far more complex in action than individual one-to-one coaching because there are more fundamental issues to be considered. Each team member arrives to team coaching with different thoughts, feelings, energy and history. Inclusion can be used in team coaching as a lens to create a greater sense of belonging, connectedness and psychological safety. This, combined with specific team based psychometric tools, can enhance the self-awareness and efficacy of the whole team.

› **Social network analysis.** To understand how inclusive a group or team is in reality; you can use social network analysis techniques. These methods use surveys, email, social media and other digital traffic to identify who are the key influencers in the group and who is most excluded, sitting outside of the key channels of conversation. Solutions can then be suggested to remedy imbalances in the network.

› **Executive search and recruitment.** When looking for prospective candidates for a role in your team, ensure you use diverse shortlists to make your decision. Open your mind to the identification of non-obvious backgrounds to enable a wider pool of talent to be considered, such as individuals from adjacent or completely different industries. You may benefit from blind CVs to avoid gender and racial bias. You may also consider removing the names of academic establishments to avoid educational elitism. As best you can, try to consider a wider spectrum of candidate, whilst considering the specific industry and geographical region you are in and adjusting your expectations in line with the talent market.

CULTURE

› **Leadership events.** Events can signal a cultural change and are unique opportunities to reinforce I&D principles. The focus should be less on getting a keynote speaker to inspire everyone and more on transformational experiences that get individuals to reflect deeply and consider how they can be culture creators rather than passive players.

› **Virtual working policy and training.** Contribute to the development and launch of agreed principles and practices regarding virtual working and how it can be delivered inclusively. On the one hand, virtual working provides greater access and opportunities to those excluded previously from the job market, such as the disabled, those with mental health challenges or neuro-diverse conditions. However, virtual working conditions also place a lot of stress on employees from different socio-economic backgrounds and for those with families and those without for different reasons. The mental health challenges for your team around isolation and loneliness need to be considered seriously, as well as the benefits of less travelling time and more family time.

› **Global culture change programmes.** The organisation with your support, commits to delivering global sessions across the employee base so that there is a shared language and understanding of I&D and leadership. Special additional sessions can be run for senior leaders and those with line manager responsibilities to further embed learning and enable a cultural shift at the senior end.

› **Inclusion and diversity champion community.** Consider building a community of individuals at all levels who are committed to going above and beyond their day jobs to create an inclusive culture. The group should aim to drive change at group, regional and local levels, ensuring both alignment and momentum, especially when budgets may be limited.

BRAND

› **Digital media and social networks.** Influence your organisation's external marketing and communications efforts to utilise video content, blogs and social networks to create conversation and build interest, raise awareness and get commitment. Consider how you can engage internal influencers to focus outward to shift perceptions and build presence in diverse communities.

› **Corporate Social Responsibility (CSR) initiatives.** Assist your organisation to identify CSR opportunities that really make a difference to create social change in local and regional communities but which, at the same time, help people feel a sense of contribution and impact by enabling them to get personally involved.

› **Brand activism.** Support your organisation to get behind a social issue that has both business strategic importance and ethical weight. This may be connected to reducing social inequity in society, investing money in specific social causes or influencing policy at a governmental level.

Measurement and Analytics

Inclusion and diversity can be measured using quantitative and qualitative methods, from engagement surveys and questionnaires to focus groups and interviews. Internal metrics such as recruitment, performance, promotion and exit interview data needs to be captured. This, combined with external data from industry benchmarks, Glassdoor and brand indexes, provides a fuller picture of the current state and progression of your organisation over time.

Measurement requires you to capture as much data as possible across visible and non-visible elements of diversity to identify the fairness of processes across the employee lifecycle. However, GDPR has made this process more difficult as organisations feel unable to request this information; beyond gender, very little information is mined. Also, due to historic disadvantage and societal stigmatisation, individuals sometimes refuse to share personal information, such as specific types of neurodiversity or ethnicity, in case of judgement. Without the data you cannot identify and understand the pinch points that lead to exclusion.

To quota or not to quota, that is the question

Positive discrimination, also known as affirmative action, is where an employer gives preferential treatment to a candidate based on their protected characteristic (e.g. gender, ethnicity, etc.). Although illegal in the UK, due to quotas being instigated in the US where it is legal, positive discrimination is becoming more acceptable.

In contrast, positive action is legal in the UK and is within the range of government measures designed to reduce discrimination in the workplace under the Equality Act 2010. It can be used in two areas: 'encouragement and training' and 'recruitment and promotion'. For example, where two candidates are of equal qualification, the individual from the under-represented group can be chosen.

I think organisations are often pushing positive discrimination to look good in the eyes of others, rather than investing the time and energy it takes to implement positive action. I would suggest that quotas come with an organisational health warning. They can drive the wrong behaviours, especially if tied to remuneration or enhancing personal image in the organisation. They can encourage superficial diversity without authentic cultural change.

There is a difference between aspirations, targets and quotas. Aspirations are good intentions and rarely lead to change and quotas drive individuals to 'game the system', I think targets are the middle ground where goals are set and supported with tangible action taken, but without forcing in diversity prematurely. That is why in parallel it is so important to measure inclusion at the individual, team and culture level. This can be done by utilising performance management, 360, pulse and engagement surveys and culture diagnostics.

Profit, people and planet

In 1994, John Elkington, the famed British management consultant and sustainability guru, coined the phrase 'triple bottom line' (TBL), designed to examine a company's social, environment, and economic impact. The idea was that organisations should be dedicated to not just be 'best in the world' but 'best for the world.' They need to be led not to maximise profit, but to find the optimal balance between profit, people and planet.

I believe if we are to create sustainable change over the long-term, leaders and organisations need to be held to account and that is why ESG (environmental, social and corporate governance) goals are vital. They communicate the ambitions of the organisation's strategy and hold leaders to account in the eyes of investors and wider society. When they are managed well, ESG goals create business value and shift perceptions about a brand.

A key challenge of the TBL, according to Elkington, is the difficulty of measuring the social and environmental bottom lines. Profitability is inherently quantitative, so it is easy to measure. What constitutes social and environmental responsibility, however, is somewhat subjective. How do you put a dollar value on an oil spill—or on preventing one—for example? Profits matter in the triple bottom line—just not at the expense of social and environmental concerns. A long-term lens in business is required that considers not just hitting financial results today, but leaving a legacy that future generations can benefit from too.

THE INCLUSIVE LEADER SCORECARD

Take a look at the Inclusive Leader Scorecard and pull together all your scores from the previous chapters under 'My Current Reality' circle. This is the current map of where your strength and development areas are.

MY CURRENT REALITY

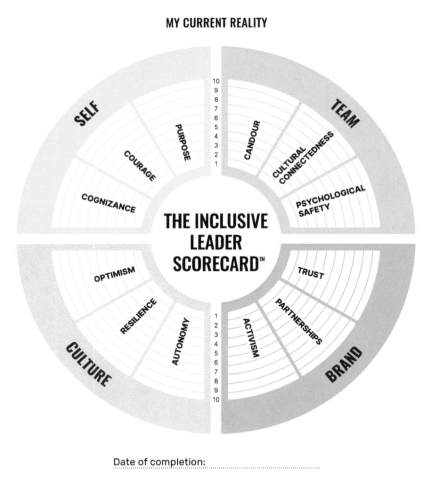

Date of completion:

PULLING IT ALL TOGETHER

Consider a realistic period of time such as a year from now, where would you like to be? What is realistically achievable? Complete the 'My Aspiration' circle to represent the progress you want to make over a specified time horizon in each of the dimensions.

MY ASPIRATION

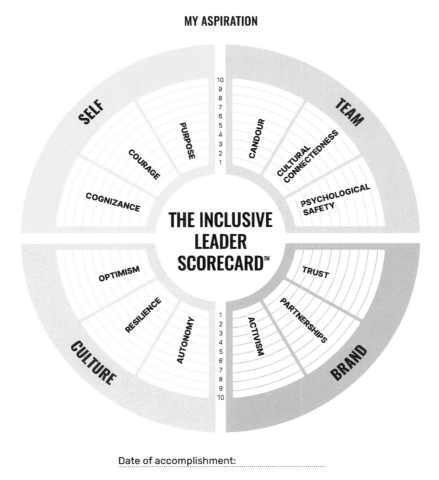

Date of accomplishment:

THE INCLUSIVE LEADER SCORECARD

To make tangible progress from your current reality towards realising your aspirations, consider in each of the quadrants why is development and growth important to you? What are the goals you want to aim for? What actions will help you to progress? What support will you need to move forward? Consider a timeframe of 6–12 months, review your learning and at the end of this period consider creating a new action plan which builds on what you have achieved.

LEADING SELF: How do I model inclusive leadership?

Why

Goals

Actions

Support

LEADING TEAM: How do I enable my team to be inclusive?

Why

Goals

Actions

Support

ACTION PLAN

LEADING CULTURE: How do I grow an inclusive culture?

Why

Goals

Actions

Support

LEADING BRAND: How do I deliver an inclusive brand?

Why

Goals

Actions

Support

KEY

Why. Why is this quadrant personally meaningful to you? What difference will progress in this area make to your leadership style?

Goals. What are the key goals you are going to commit energy, time and resource to?

Actions. Which specific actions will help you achieve your goals and live your purpose?

Support. What help, guidance, mentoring or coaching will you call upon to help you achieve progress in this quadrant?

KEY POINTS

- To progress the I&D agenda requires every leader to make a commitment to act. The Inclusive Leader Scorecard fits within a wider process of steps that enable an organisation to progress.

- The I&D discovery audit provides an honest assessment of your existing approach and makes recommendations to move forward.

- Once the here and now is clear, it is important to have a compelling vision to aim for and a strategy to get there. The leader must align their organisation's I&D vision and strategy with the overarching business and people strategy to encourage buy-in.

- A range of interventions can be taken at an organisational level to strengthen each quadrant of the Inclusive Leader Scorecard.

- I&D can be measured using quantitative and qualitative methods, from engagement surveys and questionnaires to focus groups and interviews. Internal metrics such as recruitment, performance, promotion and exit interview data need to be captured.

- The triple bottom line highlights the importance of not just measuring profit, but also considering the impact on people and the planet.

Chapter Eleven

Conclusion

The Fourth Industrial Revolution is about more than just technology-driven change; it is an opportunity to help everyone, including leaders, policy-makers and people from all income groups and nations, to harness converging technologies in order to create an inclusive, human-centred future. The real opportunity is to look beyond technology and find ways to give the greatest number of people the ability to positively impact their families, organisations and communities.

—Weforum.org

The time for talking is over. For decades, successive governments and employers have professed their commitment to equality, yet vast inequality continues to exist. This must change now. Progress in the revolutionising of inclusion and diversity works best when it involves everyone from the top down. Consequently, it must be embedded in every aspect of the organisation from senior management to grassroots. Ultimately, it has an impact on how your external brand and external stakeholders view your organisation. I&D isn't just a tick box exercise—it makes good business sense and quite frankly, it's the right and ethical thing to do for your team members, your organisation and your customers.

As we enter a post pandemic global recession, the need for inclusive leadership is critical, and we need to respond to it proactively rather than relying on outdated modes of reactivity. As we move into an ever more virtual and global workplace, the strategic business opportunities offered by I&D initiatives become essential to accomplish collective goals. It takes skill, effort and hard work to weave a cohesive I&D thread throughout an organisation rather than it being a standalone activity.

Ideally, over time the term 'I&D' will become redundant; we need to embed it within the culture and re-think our mindsets as leaders so this is just the way we do business, no special terminology required. Once you, I and others see the power of people working together without fear of unfair judgement or discrimination, we'll witness the true impact of inclusion.

We have seen how more inclusive and diverse organisations outperform their peers. However, many executive teams are less focused on the strategic I&D initiatives that can lead to these competitive advantages. It's paramount for leaders to demonstrate they understand the inclusion needs of employees, customers and society, in addition to their wants. It is essential they view I&D, not as a transactional HR process, but a business game changer.

In recognition that more needs to be done, the Inclusive Leader Scorecard offers a framework to help leaders embed I&D throughout their organisation from self, to team, to culture and to brand. The 12 individual dimensions of purpose, cognizance, courage, candour, cultural connectedness, psychological safety, optimism, resilience, autonomy, trust, partnerships and activism—all encourage leaders to reflect on their own individual practice and examine how they are responsible for enabling inclusion to flourish. In the words of Barack Obama, 'Change will not come if we wait for some other person, or if we wait for some other time. We are the ones we've been waiting for. We are the change that we seek.'

Glossary of Terms

Belonging. Belonging is a key component of inclusion. When employees are truly included, they perceive that the organisation cares for them as individuals and can share their authentic selves.

Diversity. Diversity represents the spectrum of human difference which can be identified and experienced relating to protected characteristics such as race, ethnicity and gender but also hidden differences such as neurodiversity and cultural heritage.

Equality. Equality is about ensuring everybody has an equal opportunity and is not treated differently or discriminated against because of their characteristics.

Equity. Equity refers to providing additional resources and support to those who have faced unfair discrimination, thereby enabling a level playing field. For example, equality might be providing every employee with the same technology such as a laptop, whereas equity is about adapting the technology to the needs of a disabled employee.

ERG. Employee resource groups are voluntary, employee-led groups that foster a diverse, inclusive workplace aligned with organisational mission, values, goals, business practices and objectives.

Identity. Identity is about who you are, the way you think about yourself, the way you are viewed by the world and the characteristics that define you.

Inclusion. Inclusion refers to when the human needs of feeling a sense of belonging to a group and need to be acknowledged for one's unique contribution is fulfilled.

Intersectionality. The term 'intersectionality' was coined in 1989 by professor Kimberlé Crenshaw to describe how race, class, gender, and other identities 'intersect' with one another and overlap. The intersection of some of these identities impact the way we are perceived and treated and in turn, influence the way individuals engage with the world around them.

Lived experience. Lived experience refers to the subjective representation an individual forms about past events in their lives which inform and influence the choices they have made and continue to make.

These are often centred around specific identities of importance (e.g. ethnicity, gender, sexuality, etc.).

Positive action. Positive action refers to providing additional support and guidance to address any imbalance of opportunity those with a protected characteristic may face such as career guidance, CV clinics, etc., but ultimately the individual goes through the same process of selection as everyone else.

Positive discrimination. Positive discrimination refers to the act of giving advantage and preferential treatment to those groups in society who have been treated unfairly due to their protected characteristic, such as by enabling individuals to bypass certain criteria or stages in a selection process.

Privilege. Privilege refers to a right, immunity, or benefit enjoyed by a particular person or a restricted group of people beyond the advantages of others.

Psychological safety. Psychological safety is being able to show and employ oneself without fear of negative consequences to self-image or status. It can be defined as a shared belief that interpersonal risk taking is safe and encouraged.

References

Chapter One
Books

Darwin, C. (1859), *Origin of the Species*, John Murray.

Darwin, C. (1871), *The Descent of Man*, John Murray.

Schwab, K. (2016), *The Fourth Industrial Revolution*, Penguin Random House.

Websites

Cowen, A. (2005), *Are the Wealthy More Narcissistic?* Available at: https://matrix.berkeley.edu/research/are-wealthy-more-narcissistic (Accessed: 4 Dec 2020)

United Nations Global Impact (2017), *Bloomberg LP Impact Report 2018*. Available at: https://www.unglobalcompact.org/participation/report/cop/create-and-submit/active/427860 (Accessed: 4 Dec 2020)

Wilson, N. (2019), *Ten Guidelines for Inclusive Capitalism*. Available at: https://www.legalandgeneralgroup.com/media-centre/blogs/ten-guidelines-for-inclusive-capitalism (Accessed: 4 Dec 2020)

Chapter Two
Books

Adler, A. (2010), reprint, *Understanding the Human Nature*, Martino Fine Books.

Syed, M. (2020), *Rebel Ideas: The Power of Diverse Thinking*, John Murray.

Websites

Dishman, L. (2015), *The Business Case for Women in the C-Suite*. Available at: https://www.fastcompany.com/3048342/the-business-case-for-women-in-the-c-suite (Accessed: 4 Dec 2020)

Dixon-Fyle, S. Dolan, K. Hunt, V. & Prince, S. (2020), *Diversity Wins: How Inclusion Matters*. Available at: https://www.mckinsey.com/featured-insights/diversity-and-inclusion/diversity-wins-how-inclusion-matters (Accessed: 4 Dec 2020)

Glassdoor (2014), *Two-thirds of People Consider Diversity Important when Deciding where to Work, Glassdoor Survey*. Available at: https://www.glassdoor.com/about-us/twothirds-people-diversity-important-deciding-work-glassdoor-survey-2/ (Accessed: 4 Dec 2020)

Gompers, P. & Kovvali, S. (2018), *The Other Diversity Dividend*. Available at: https://hbr.org/2018/07/the-other-diversity-dividend (Accessed: 4 Dec 2020)

Lorenzo, R. Voigt, N. Schetelig, K. Zawadzki, A. Welpe, I. & Brosi, P. (2017), *The Mix that Matters*. Available at: https://www.bcg.com/publications/2017/people-organization-leadership-talent-innovation-through-diversity-mix-that-matters (Accessed: 4 Dec 2020)

Lorenzo, R, Voigt, N. Tsusaka, M. Krentz, M. & Abouzahr, K. (2018), *How Diverse Leadership Boosts Innovation*. Available at: https://www.bcg.com/en-us/publications/2018/how-diverse-leadership-teams-boost-innovation (Accessed: 4 Dec 2020)

Chapter Three

Journals

Brewer, M.B. (1991), The Social Self: on being the same and different at the same time. *Personality and Social Psychology Bulletin*, 17 (5), pp. 475-482.

Websites

Coaston, J. (2019), *The Intersectionality Wars*. Available at: https://www.vox.com/the-highlight/2019/5/20/18542843/intersectionality-conservatism-law-race-gender-discrimination (Accessed: 4 Dec 2020)

H.M. Government (2015), *Equality Act Guidance 2010*. Available at: https://www.gov.uk/guidance/equality-act-2010-guidance (Accessed: 4 Dec 2020)

Chapter Four

Websites

Sweet, J. & Shook, E. (2020), *Getting to Equal 2020, The Hidden Value of Culture Makers*. Available at: https://www.accenture.com/_acnmedia/Thought-Leadership-Assets/PDF-2/Accenture-Getting-To-Equal-2020-Research-Report.pdf (Accessed: 4 Dec 2020)

Chapter Five

Books

Deal, T. & Kennedy, A. (1982), *Corporate Cultures: The Rites and Rituals of Corporate Life*, Addison Publishing Co.

Websites

Re:Work Guides (2020), *Understand Team Effectiveness*. Available at: https://rework.withgoogle.com/print/guides/5721312655835136/ (Accessed: 4 Dec 2020)

Chapter Six

Books

Brown, B. (2015), *Daring Greatly*, Avery Books.

Kahneman, D. et al (2002), ed. *Heuristics and Biases: The Psychology of Intuitive Judgement*, Cambridge University Press.

Thompson, L. (2010), 4th ed. *Making the Team: A Guide for Managers*, Pearson College Division.

Websites

Buster, B. (2020), *Cognitive Biases: A cheat sheet to help you remember 200+ biases via 3 conundrums*. Blog. Available at: https://busterbenson.com/piles/cognitive-biases/ (Accessed: 4 Dec 2020)

Heick, T. (2019), *The Cognitive Bias Codex: A Visual of 180+ Cognitive Biases*. Available at: https://www.teachthought.com/critical-thinking/the-cognitive-bias-codex-a-visual-of-180-cognitive-biases/ (Accessed: 4 Dec 2020)

Linkedin (2017), *Purpose at Work, 2016 Global Report*. Available at: https://business.linkedin.com/content/dam/me/business/en-us/talent-solutions/resources/pdfs/purpose-at-work-global-report.pdf (Accessed: 4 Dec 2020)

Chapter Seven

Books and Journals

Edmondson, A. 1999. Psychological Safety and Learning Behaviour in Work Teams. *Administrative Science Quarterly*, 44 (2): 350–383.

Meyer, E. (2014), *Culture Map: Breaking Through the Invisible Boundaries of Global Business*, Public Affairs.

Travis, Shaffer, and Thorpe-Moscon, (2019), *Getting Real About Inclusive Leadership: Why Change Starts With You*, Catalyst.

Welch, J. & Welch, S. (2006), *Winning*, Harper International.

Websites

Blakely, J. (2015), *The Support/Challenge Matrix: Coaching Moments of Choice*. Available at: https://trustedexecutive.com/the-support-challenge-matrix-coaching-moments-of-choice/ (Accessed: 4 Dec 2020)

Phillips. K. (2014), *How Diversity Makes us Smarter*. Available at: https://www.scientificamerican.com/article/how-diversity-makes-us-smarter/ (Accessed: 4 Dec 2020)

Ripmeester, N. (2015), *We all Speak English, don't we?* Available at: https://www.linkedin.com/pulse/we-all-speak-english-dont-nannette-ripmeester (Accessed: 4 Dec 2020)

Chapter Eight

Books

Deal, T. & Kennedy, A. (1982), *Corporate Cultures: The Rites and Rituals of Corporate Life*, Addison Publishing Co.

Pink, D. (2011), *Drive: The Surprising Truth About What Motivates Us*, Riverside Books

Seligman, M. (1990), *Learned Optimism*, Vintage Books.

Zautra, A. J., Hall, J. S., & Murray, K. E. (2010). Resilience: A new definition of health for people and communities. In: Reich, J, W., Zautra. A. J., & Hall, J. S. *Handbook of Adult Resilience*. The Guildford Press.

Websites

Ariely, D. Gneezy, D. Loewenstein, G. & Mazar, N. (2005*), Large Stakes and Big Mistakes*. Available at: http://citeseerx.ist.psu.edu/viewdoc/download?doi=10.1.1.362.1828&rep=rep1&type=pdf (Accessed: 4 Dec 2020)

Blackrock (2020), *Resilience Amid Uncertainty*. Available at: https://www.blackrock.com/corporate/about-us/sustainability-resilience-research (Accessed: 4 Dec 2020)

Deci, E. (1971), *Effects of Externally Mediated Rewards on Intrinsic Motivation*. Available at: https://selfdeterminationtheory.org/SDT/documents/1971_Deci.pdf (Accessed: 4 Dec 2020)

Hemel, G & Zanini, M. (2020), *Harnessing Everyday Genius*. Available at: https://hbr.org/2020/07/harnessing-everyday-genius (Accessed: 4 Dec 2020)

Reeves, M. & Whitaker, K. A *Guide to Building a More Resilient Business.* Available at: https://hbr.org/2020/07/a-guide-to-building-a-more-resilient-business (Accessed: 4 Dec 2020)

Stockholm Resilience Centre (2018), *What is Resilience? An Introduction to a Popular yet often Misunderstood Concept*. Available at: https://www.stockholmresilience.org/research/research-news/2015-02-19-what-is-resilience.html (Accessed: 4 Dec 2020)

Chapter Nine

Books and Journals

Drucker, P (1946), *The Concept of the Corporation*, John Day Co.

Green, C. Maister, D. & Galford, R. (2006), *The Trusted Advisor*, Tantor Media.

Lazarsfield, P. & Merton, R. (1954), Friendship as a Social Process: a substantive and methodological analysis. In *Freedom and Control in Modern Society*, ed. Berger, M. pp. 18-66, NY, Van Nostrand.

Kotler, P. & Sarkar, C. (2018), *Brand Activism for Purpose to Action*, Idea Bite Press.

Websites

Activistbrands (2020), *What is Brand Activism?* Available at: http://www.activistbrands.com/what-is-brand-activism/ (Accessed: 4 Dec 2020)

Brandfog (2018), *CEOs Speaking Out on Social Media Survey*. Available at: https://brandfog.com/survey/2018_ceo_survey.pdf (Accessed: 4 Dec 2020)

Edelman, (2020), *2020 Edelman Trust Barometer*. Available at: https://www.edelman.com/trustbarometer (Accessed: 4 Dec 2020)

Edelman, (2020), *Trust Barometer Special Report: Brand Trust in 2020*. Available at: https://www.edelman.com/research/brand-trust-2020 (Accessed: 4 Dec 2020)

Frei, F & Morriss, A. (2020), *Begin with Trust*. Available at: https://hbr. org/2020/05/begin-with-trust (Accessed: 4 Dec 2020)

Godin, S. (2009), *Define: Brand*, blog. Available at: https://seths. blog/2009/12/define-brand/ (Accessed: 4 Dec 2020)

Interbrand (2019), *Best Global Brands 2019*. Available at: https://www. interbrand.com/best-brands/best-global-brands/2019/download/ (Accessed: 4 Dec 2020)

Ipsos (2018), *What Worries the World – Sept 2018*. Available at: https:// www.ipsos.com/en/what-worries-world-september-2018 (Accessed: 4 Dec 2020)

Kotler, P. & Sarker, C. (2018), *The Case for Brand Activism*. Available at: https://www.marketingjournal.org/the-case-for-brand-activism-a-discussion-with-philip-kotler-and-christian-sarkar/ (Accessed: 4 Dec 2020)

United Nations (2015), *Sustainable Development Goals*. Available at: https://www.undp.org/content/undp/en/home/sustainable-development-goals.html (Accessed: 4 Dec 2020)

Chapter Ten

Websites

Bartlett, E. (2011), *Legal Q&A: Positive Action under the Equality Act 2010*. Available at: https://www.personneltoday.com/hr/legal-qa-positive-action-under-the-equality-act-2010/ (Accessed: 4 Dec 2020)

Elkington, J. (2018), *25 Years Ago I Coined the Phrase "Triple Bottom Line." Here's Why it's Time to Rethink it*. Available at: https://hbr. org/2018/06/25-years-ago-i-coined-the-phrase-triple-bottom-line-heres-why-im-giving-up-on-it (Accessed: 4 Dec 2020)

CPSIA information can be obtained
at www.ICGtesting.com
Printed in the USA
BVHW021710100221
599843BV00007B/31